Life Prescription

John Mauldin, Ph.D.

KENDALL/HUNT PUBLISHING COMPANY
4050 Westmark Drive   Dubuque, Iowa 52002

This book is dedicated to my parents
John T. Mauldin, Sr. and
Anne Scott Harman Mauldin.

Copyright ©1997 Mauldin Consulting Group, John Mauldin, President

Library of Congress Card Catalog Number: 96-77164

ISBN 0-7872-2456-1

All rights reserved. No part of this publication may be reproduced, stored in a retrieval system, or transmitted, in any form or by any means, electronic, mechanical, photocopying, recording, or otherwise, without the prior written permission of the copyright owner.

Printed in the United States of America

10 9 8 7 6 5 4 3 2 1

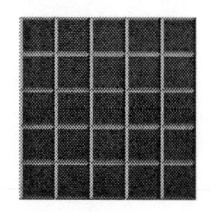

Contents

Acknowledgments   v
Introduction: What's This All About?   vii

Chapter 1   Why Do I Do the Things I Do?   1
Chapter 2   Why Do We Need Patterns?   7
Chapter 3   Beginning Patterns   13
Chapter 4   A Patterning Process   17
Chapter 5   Patterning Process: Problem, Orientation, Testing   23
Chapter 6   Patterning Process: Learning from Adult Patterns   29
Chapter 7   Patterning Process: Rules   39
Chapter 8   Pattern Operation   47
Chapter 9   Pattern Operation and Motivation   55
Chapter 10   Pattern Operation and Dynamic Attractors   61
Chapter 11   Pattern Operation: Power and Change   67
Chapter 12   Patterns Uncovered and the Battle Within   75
Chapter 13   Building Healthy or Unhealthy Patterns   85
Chapter 14   A Healthy Pattern Process in Life   93
Chapter 15   The Big Picture   103

References   113

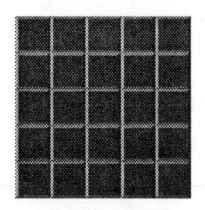

Acknowledgments

I have wanted to write this book for more than 15 years. It took the concerted support of many people to produce the final work. I want to thank Dr. Nina Dulin-Mallory for her patient editing and insights into the content, which kept me excited about the work. I want to thank my parents, who gave me *my* patterns and the abilities to understand patterns. Thanks to all the people who were willing to suffer through the first readings and give me their comments: Creighton Kelly, Dr. John Mauldin Sr., Anne Scott Mauldin, Betsy Kourkounis, Terri Buckland, Regenia Andrews, and James Cardwell. Particular thanks for their patience goes to my wife, Jeannie, and son, Randall, who endured all my hours at the computer.

My greatest appreciation goes to Regenia, Betsy, and James who pushed me to finish, supported me during the work, and suffered all the false starts and anticipation with me.

Introduction:
What's This All About?

Most of us spend a great deal of our time in a general search for meaning. What does it mean when the boss calls you to her office? What does it mean when your parents die? Just who is John Gault? As human beings, we seek to know how the coin machine operates when we want a drink, how people operate in our lives, and how the universe operates.

Searching for meaning causes us headaches, but on occasion we find what we are seeking and feel relieved. We discover where the water leak is coming from, we design a business system that truly works, or we understand someone's actions a little better after talking to him. After working with people for years, I find that we are all seeking a way to make sense of our world.

Beginning at birth, we are challenged to learn how the parts of our world fit together and how we fit into it. This challenge is not idle. A child's survival depends on knowing what is dangerous. To thrive, children must understand both dangers and delights. Learning from their parents, children can navigate difficult waters to gain control of their lives as an adult.

Introduction

In the midst of control lies a pattern—a mosaic used to negotiate life's waters. A pattern acts as a map to aide us in finding successful paths and meanings within life. The pattern can be simple or complex. For example, men normally carry their wallets in the same pocket all their life. This custom is so predictable that some clothing manufacturers put a button on the back left pocket of men's pants, but not on the back right pocket.

Once these patterns are formed, adults do not think about them. They act and react to a meaning-filled dance. They could adapt differently. Change could be a friend without mystery, but its steps are a new pattern. Doing new actions, unfamiliar to us, causes stress. Why revisit a struggle for meaning when what I know works well enough for me today? And yet some aspects of our lives *don't* work—a marriage, a relationship with a child, a work environment, an attitude, a behavior—and as long as the pattern we use to solve our problems doesn't change, the outcome doesn't change either. We create our patterns. We control and keep them in place for our pleasure or pain.

This book presents a systematic way of looking at people, their patterns, pattern change, and the effect of patterns in systems, such as business and government. People are predictable. They follow rules of operation that can be understood by anyone. The rules are not obscure, but clear. *Each outcome of a pattern recreates the reason for its existence.* Every ounce of energy spent in producing the pattern's actions makes sense to the person who develops the pattern. Any challenge to a person's existing pattern is met with forceful resistance.

In our times, many people are looking for greater meaning in their lives. This book is a beginning.

CHAPTER • 1

Why Do I Do the Things I Do?

We all enter the world as children, helpless and useless. Starting out in such a slow way, having no control, we turn out nicely for the most part. The process of becoming a thinking adult is no small matter, and we are required to rethink our journey from time to time. The process should be more understandable. But most of us remember little about the process of maturation, and many do not want to relive it. Why would we want to return to a time when we did not have control of our bodies, much less our lives?

If developmentalists are to be believed, children are great problem-solvers. They do not solve problems the same way you and I do. Instead, they are naturals, working from instinct to formulate solutions. From experience, I can attest that this is true. Let me give you a couple of examples. A father who made his living as a truck driver was on the road two to three weeks at a time. When he came home, he and his wife wanted some quiet time in the bedroom. Their four-year-old would come down the hall, sit in front of the bedroom door, and bang her head against it. The parents were concerned with her actions and they brought the child to me for help. What we discovered was that the child's interpretation and what was really happening were not the same. The parents did not think the child could hear them, but the child told me that she thought her mother was being hurt. She could only think of one thing to do to stop her mother from being hurt—to bang her head on the door until she hurt herself. Her action stopped the mother's cries and brought her mother to her. The solution worked. The child caused herself pain to solve the problem of her mother's (supposed) pain.

Next, an eighteen-month-old child sat and played happily in the corner of a room while his mother was being interviewed. During the interview, the mother began to cry and the baby crawled across the room and climbed into the mother's lap. She was distracted by the child sitting in her lap and stopped crying. As soon as the mother stopped crying, the baby climbed down and began to play again. This series of actions was repeated every time the mother cried.

In both of these examples, a child saw a problem. Each interpreted what would affect the problem and acted accordingly. In both cases, the problem was solved. A mother came out of a room where she was being "hurt," and a distracted mother regained emotional control.

Workable Solutions

Workable solutions begin when a child is faced with an upset parent, a busy intersection, a barking dog, or anything that does not readily make sense. "Not making sense" may mean that an event is a real trauma or just an unexpected occurrence. While a wet diaper is a serious discomfort to a baby, adults do not consider it serious. Everybody goes through some discomfort in life. The successful negotiation of a discomfort and making sense of it shape the actions that people take in later life.

Children work the hardest to make sense of problems. If they encounter distress in life, they create a way to problem-solve it. The eighteen-month-old whose mother was crying focused his parent's emotions by distracting her from her sadness. This early solution can reemerge in later life when, for example, this child cares for an emotionally disabled parent or wife. In a different scenario, a parent was abusive toward a child's older siblings. The child discovered a hiding place where the parent could not reach him. When the cues of abuse began, this child ran away and climbed into his hiding place, even though he was not the focus of the abuse. Later, as an adult, during times of psychological distress, he would exhibit similar behavior, leaving a partner after causing a disturbance with her. After the fight, he had an excuse to run from the relationship. This maneuver pulled him safely from a potentially abusive situation.

What a person does to solve a problem as a child is exactly what he will do to solve a problem as an adult. If I run away as a child, I will run away as an adult. I may run differently, but I still run away. If I solve a problem by consoling a person as a child, then I will console people as I grow up. If I solve a problem by becoming angry or explosive or forcing people to attend to me, then I will become angry or explosive or force people to deal with me when I am an adult. These actions are patterns from childhood applied in an adult setting.

What Are Patterns?

Patterns are systematic ways of negotiating life that can be seen in a person's actions. They are systematic because they have a distinct beginning, process, and end. The beginning of a pattern occurs when a person needs an exact way to negotiate a problem or situation. It ends when his actions produce an expected conclusion that is satisfactory to the pattern owner. The actions taken in the process are specific to what the individual believes will produce success.

A natural analogy for patterns is a stream. If you go high enough into the mountains and find the beginning of a stream, you will see that the water takes a particular path, working its way down the mountain. As it moves, it gathers force. Year after year when the rains fall, the stream takes the same path. The greater the force of the water, the less things can stand in its way. It erodes banks that try to hold it. It sweeps into cracks and weakens structures until they crumble into the water and are swept away. Likewise, people devise actions that take a predictable course and resist changes in that course. Like the stream, people problem-solve obstacles to their chosen course. In both cases, the result is a measurable, predictable, patterned process.

The Need for a Pattern

The rain, stream, riverbed, and river follow a course. They operate in an understandable and predictable manner. Neither the course nor its function deviate much. If there is no rain, there is little force to the river. If there is heavy rain, there is greater force. People are the same. The energy they use to problem-solve the issues they face in their lives is consistent with the degree of success they feel they will have. They invent, discover, and develop patterns of problem-solving from which they rarely deviate, and which they believe to be the best way to solve their problems.

People develop their problem-solving patterns when they face problems. The age of development equals the sophistication of the pattern. Maturity is hard-won. The struggle to master problem-solving frightens most of us and stops our search for new or different approaches. We desist because we reach a place of security—a comfort zone where we have control and can predict most events around us. We build a house, have a good job, and find comfort in our relationships with friends and family. Herein is the greatest paradox: As our comfort is based on our feeling all-knowing and all-powerful, we create a place where we have control and enjoy the predictability of coming events. We expect the events of the world to pass by us without causing grief. But this expectation that the world will run along our personal river channel and leave us alone is false.

The creation of a pattern to live inside, like a cocoon, denies that predators are present. It denies that we are human and are participants in a bigger cycle—a cycle of life and a pattern of respect for the nature of the world and its operation. We can exist without acknowledging that we are part of a bigger pattern, but our existence is vague and without meaning. In denying that we are a small cog in a big system, we lose the ability to problem-solve new issues that arise. For example, our society has lost the ability to problem-solve how to teach our children, and so we have a failed educational system. We have lost the ability to manage our money, to manage our children, and to manage our lives. It is past time to regain control of our problem-solving ability and create a system where the inmates are not running the asylum.

The goal of this book is to offer an understanding of patterns, pattern development, and how to manage personal growth, so that the spark of innovative and intelligent problem-solving is not lost in the weight of apathy. We all have ability. Most people want to live strong, consistent, supportive lives. Knowing what to do and how to do it is the art of managing your life.

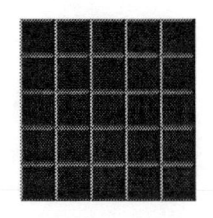

CHAPTER • 2

Why Do We Need Patterns?

As Children, Parents Solve Our Problems

Children enter the world shoeless and clueless. Our predicament at birth is that we cannot fulfill our own needs. We require help just to survive. We are completely dependent on other people and have no base of knowledge about what is going on around us. We receive much attention, but can give very little in return.

Starting life in this precarious position, babies require care before they are able to care for themselves. Parental actions may both predict and respond to the needs of a baby. If a baby has a wet diaper, a parent may either anticipate the need to change it or wait until the baby announces it.

The degree of preparation and thought the parent gives to solving the baby's problem falls into a range of care, which can vary greatly. A parent may attend to every whimper, or not respond until the distress is deafening. The basic idea is that *the development of any child starts with the adult action pattern that produces need fulfillment.* The action pattern parents use is directly associated with the action pattern they experienced as children.

Life Prescription

A Child Adjusts to Parents' Care

Let's take an example of an adult action pattern and how it is taught to children. A frustrated husband once brought his wife to a clinic, begging for help. She was obsessed with keeping the house clean. Particularly, she did not allow anything to be laid on the bed. If anything was placed on the bed, she screamed at the offender, demanding the object be removed immediately. During counseling, we discovered that she could not remember a point in her life when it was acceptable to lay things on the bed. Her mother would punish her severely if she did not keep things off her bed. She did not know the reason for this requirement, because her mother had never told her.

The woman's mother was brought into the session and asked the same questions. The mother responded that she didn't know why she was not supposed to lay things on the bed, but her own mother was extremely strict on this point, and as a child she was punished if she laid anything on the bed.

Finally, the grandmother, now in her nineties, came to discuss the situation. She was very bright, alert, and eager to help. When asked the same questions, her first response was surprise. She said that she routinely placed things on the bed and did not understand all the fuss. When asked if there was ever a time that this was not permitted, she said, "Of course, but only for hats and coats!"

When asked why, she knew immediately. She said, "We lived in a poor section of town, and some of the children that my daughter played with had head lice. If the children came in and threw their coats on the bed, the lice would get in the bed and we would have to burn the bed and bed sheets. During the depression years, we could not afford a new mattress. I had to be very careful *never* to let the children put coats or hats on the beds." The grandmother was utterly amazed that her daughter and granddaughter had continued this practice.

In this example, the actions of the grandmother survived unexplained through two generations. To the daughter, the action had become a pattern that she taught to the granddaughter. Had the granddaughter's husband not challenged the practice, it may have continued indefinitely. No distress occurred until somebody challenged the pattern. As in this example, a developing child learns from action patterns used by adults, eventually adapting these patterns in her own actions.

Children Understand Action

Years ago, the song "Cat's In The Cradle," by Harry Chapin, made some fathers address their guilt about their relationships with their sons. The song pointed out how "sowing" non-participation with a child lets the parent "reap" non-participation when the child is grown. "I'd love to, Dad, if I could find the time. But the new job's a hassle, and the kids are in school, but it's sure nice talking to you, Dad." This response is the same as that given to the son as he grew up. *Children see, not the intent of an action, but the action itself.* Working to provide for college is not understood, throwing a ball is.

An infant needs to trust that its needs will be fulfilled. Trust is formed by specific actions, responses to specific needs. The needs are not complicated—food, shelter, warmth, and cleanliness—not complicated, but very specific. Children build patterns from the specific actions offered by their parents. *The way a parent solves a child's problem becomes the starting point for how the child will solve problems later on.* As parents, we have all said, "I swore when I was growing up I would never talk to my children the way my parents talked to me. But just today, I was saying to my son exactly what my father used to say to me." The pattern of parenting we learned is the way our parents solved the problem of being parents. Their solution was our action starting point: whatever they gave to us as specific actions is what we learned.

Parent's actions take on further significance, if they act consistently. "I will fix your drink as soon as I get off the phone," says a father. If he fixes the drink when the phone conversation is over, the child will learn to wait. If the drink is not fixed, the child will learn how to push the parent to do what he said—to be consistent. It may mean whining, or tugging, or a tantrum, whatever it takes to get the action done. Over time, such actions are built into a consistent, supported way of behavior used by both parent and child.

How did those women learn that nothing was to be laid on the bed, and then believe it so strongly that they continued the action despite no real evidence that it was the proper thing to do? To understand, we must look at pattern development as a process. This process is a specific, consistent, systematic operation with clear and definable steps. The steps are like the steps of a dance. All participants follow the steps as prescribed and in precisely the same order.

Pattern Development Process

To clarify this process further, it can be described as two ranges of operation. The first concerns relationships, and the primary relationship is between the parent and child. In the earliest stages, the parent completely controls this relationship. The child is dependent on the other person in the relationship for all his need fulfillment. Over time, this interaction will change. The child will learn to problem-solve taking care of himself. So in the first range, the control shift for the child is from others' fulfilling his needs to his own self-fulfillment.

The second range of operation concerns events in the environment. A child cannot control or avoid events in his world. They just happen, and the parent must address them. If a toddler's diaper is uncomfortable, the parent must change it. The toddler may learn to remove a diaper, but she doesn't have the skill to replace it with a fresh one. As a result, the child's control range over environmental events is nil in the earliest stages but she takes on independent action as she grows.

We can see this graphically in the following diagram:

Why Do We Need Patterns?

Child Pattern Development

Other Control of Relationships

Dependent Control of Events

Independent Control of Events

Control of relationships

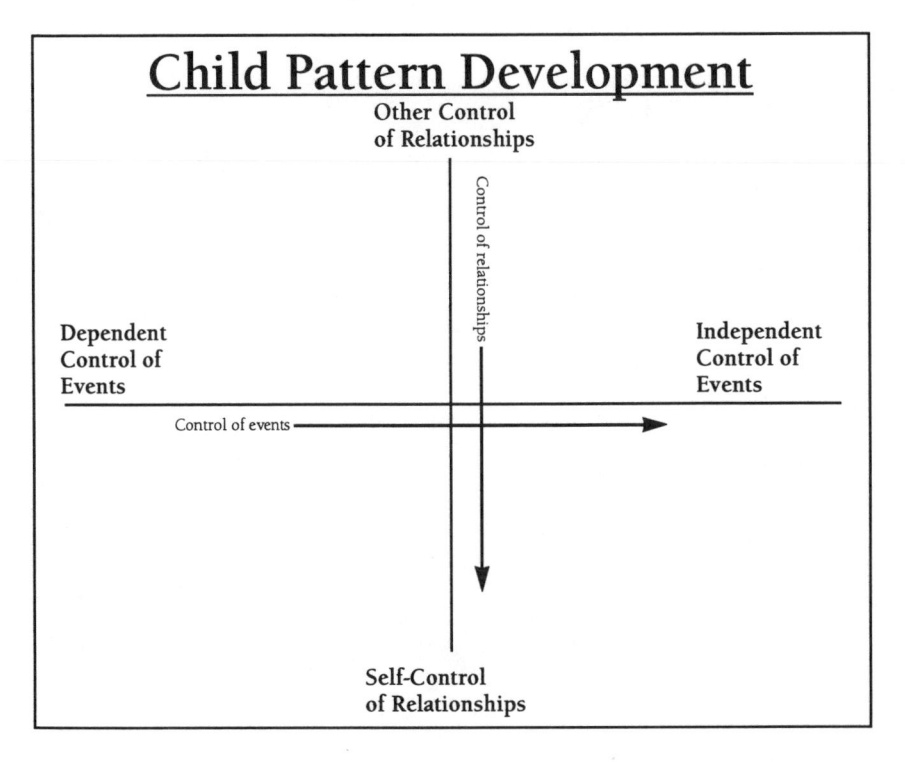

Control of events →

Self-Control of Relationships

This diagram shows that a child begins life in the upper-left quadrant and ends it in the lower right. Along the way, she develops solutions to the events and people in her environment.

CHAPTER • 3

Beginning Patterns

The proof of patterns is in the everyday reality of our actions. Take bathing. Think about getting into the shower. You reach up with the same hand, get the soap, and begin to wash in the same place every day. When applying makeup, women generally start at the same place on their face. These simple examples show how we pattern actions so that we do not have to think about them every time we act.

So patterns are everywhere, and it is important to understand how patterns operate, *for* us and *on* us. All patterns are based on individual problem-solving. At a given age, based on the data available, a child problem-solves situations that occur daily in his life. He learns early solutions from the way the most significant people in his environment problem-solve, or he may reject solutions he witnesses because of the impact he sees them having on others. In one family, the oldest child regularly helped put an alcoholic aunt to bed when she was drunk. From this experience, he determined never to drink himself.

In the development of patterns, opportunity and capacity are of equal importance. Opportunity comes when a child sees a wide range of problems solved or is helped to see variations that would improve the problem-solving process. A three-year-old child, for example, angrily demanded that her parents make the older children stop casting her as the baby when they played house. Her initial solution was to stop playing with the others. After a talk with her parents, three other solutions came to light. Not making the decision for her, the child's parents gave her new data on which to base her decision. She decided to tell the others that she would not play with them if they did not let her play other roles. The older children thought that she liked to play the baby, and they were willing to change when they knew her real feelings.

Giving multiple choices to a three-year-old seems unusual, but children gain confidence when their solutions work in the world. The solution the child chose was not part of her original discussion with her parents; rather it was a combination of options that the child created. It was her solution and it worked for her.

The second issue of importance is genetic capacity. How bright is a child? If a child is not average in intelligence, then his ability to learn problem-solving methods is restricted. In no way does this mean he cannot learn; it just takes longer and he will retain less. Parents and teachers of handicapped children have to be very specific and clear about what they are teaching these children so that it can become a consistent pattern.

In the earliest stages, specific, consistent actions come from few people—usually parents. But a child soon comes into contact with teachers, grandparents, and other caretakers. Children live in a quickly expanding world, and other people besides parents begin to give instruction and present them with problems to be solved. For example, a child came home from visiting his aunt, a woman who had a completely different child-rearing philosophy from that of his parents. She said to him, "If you act up, I'm going to sell you to the man next door." At four years old, the child did not know that this statement was only an empty threat to coerce good behavior. His parents did not use this style of control. After the aunt threatened the child, he came home very upset and afraid to go back to her house. He knew his aunt had power over him while he was in her care, and he

Beginning Patterns

was afraid that she might give him away and he would be lost to his parents. His parents could not understand his distress. Until the child realized that the aunt was not serious, he remained fearful.

I was told about a five- or six-year-old boy who liked to play in the loft of his aunt's barn. Once, when he was playing up there, his aunt told him that if she caught him there again, she would kill him. The next time he went up there to play, his aunt walked by outside. When he saw her, he got nervous and fell out of the loft. It was only about an eight-foot fall, but when he landed he started crying. His aunt ran to him to see if he was okay. He finally looked up and said, "Yeah, I'm fine, but you said you were going to kill me." He wasn't crying because he was hurt. He was crying because he was afraid that she was going to kill him.

Specific, consistent action enables a child to predict what parents will do, and what they mean by what they say. Parental actions orient the child to learn patterns. After initial orientation, children test actions on the next available person—the baby sitter, a grandparent, or anyone else. A child is continually told she is cute for pouting, but will pouting work on the teacher?

An incident that occurred after a five-year-old's mother died is a good example. When he went to the court hearing for custody between his father and grandparents, he surprised everyone by saying he would go home with his father. His older siblings knew that the father was not the best person to care for him. They went to the judge and said they did not want to have anything to do with their father. Later, I asked the five-year-old why he said he wanted to go home with his dad. He said that he was told that his mother had gone to heaven, and he wanted to go home with his dad and "wait on her to get back." He trusted that he wouldn't be with his father very long because his mother, whom he loved and cared about, was coming back from heaven. He had learned a pattern of trust. He learned this pattern from his mom; therefore, he was willing to tolerate his dad for what he thought was going to be a short period.

Patterns exist because someone believes they will work. Patterns mean the world is predictable: A is A. The creator of a pattern uses the same pattern to solve problems no matter how old he is.

CHAPTER • 4

A Patterning Process

One summer, my family was on the way back to Fripp Island in South Carolina. We stopped at a drawbridge that was open to let shrimp boats return to harbor. The skies had been threatening all day, and the first drops of rain began to hit the windshield. Without warning, a bolt of lightning hit a steel lightning rod twenty feet from our car. No one could move, because the traffic was lined up bumper to bumper. Conversation stopped as the minutes passed waiting on the bridge. Another bolt struck closer by. The cars behind us backed away. As a space opened up, I sped for it, whipping the car away from the bridge. No one spoke for several minutes, waiting for the blood flow to return. It turned out that we were not in real danger. The bridge operator told us later that it happened all the time. "Not to us," was the reply.

If we had been at home, hundreds of miles away when the lightning hit the bridge, no one would have reacted. It would have been an event without significance for us. We would not have needed to take any evasive action. An event outside my realm has limited impact on my feelings. It does not demand a decision or response. Likewise, children are not faced with learning to problem-solve events outside their realms. Events that do not directly affect them do not affect their patterns.

At night in the projects, for instance, children come in early, particularly on the weekends. These neighborhoods are the domain of drug dealers, and so children learn quickly how to avoid them. A pattern of life has developed, and parents protect their children by teaching them the rules.

On the other side of town, people congregate on the corner after their nightly walk. Parents here also want to keep their children safe, but their concerns are different. In one neighborhood it is drugs; in the other, it is teen-agers at the wheel of a speeding car. In Africa, a bushman will teach his children what snakes and animals to avoid. Survival depends on children learning how their environment works so that they can survive its dangers.

This pattern learning can be placed into a systematic process. The process is:

EVENT
FEELING
DECISION
RESPONSIBILITY
ELIMINATION

In the situation described earlier, the *event* (lightning) produced a *feeling* (fear of harm), which called for a *decision* (escape), which demanded a *response* and the *ability* to act on the response (see the opening, turn the car around), which relieved (problem-solved) and thus *eliminated* the feeling (we got out of there).

In an earlier example, three generations of normal people participated in a completely nonsensical action and forced others to participate also. Can we see a process in their actions? We can see that the *event* was "not laying things on the bed." For the grandmother, the action made perfect sense and kept the bed free from lice. It was a necessary action at the time. For the mother, the *event* did not mean anything. She was unaware of the lice factor, but the grandmother's reaction when something was laid on the bed was so severely punishing that the mother decided laying things on the bed was bad. The *feeling* she faced was a fear of her mother's reaction. She had to solve the problem so that her mother's reaction did not produce a bad feeling (anxiety) or punitive reaction (spanking). She made a *decision* not to lay things on the bed, which had to be carried out by the response she was able to produce *(responsibility)*. If she was *response-able* in not laying things on the bed, she would *eliminate* her mother's reaction and return their relationship to harmony.

Once the mother had accepted this behavior as something that worked, she never questioned whether she should teach her daughter (the granddaughter). She used the same punitive tactics that her mother had used on her. Thus, the granddaughter learned how to control her mother's anger by not laying things on the bed. In both cases where the women did not know the real reason for "not laying things on the bed," they merely *adjusted their actions to accommodate the consistent demands of the person who did*. They were not solving the problem of "laying things on the bed," they were solving the *(event)* problem of their parent's reaction. Their goal was to keep a good relationship with their parent, not to avoid lice.

Patterns exist to help people eliminate feelings or events which they are problem-solving. Patterns do not end until the event or the feeling goes away. The decision I make alleviates my distress. My decision is completely personal. It is not made for others, it is made for *me*.

All Patterns Make Sense to Their Owner

You probably know someone who always appears unsatisfied with other people's work, someone who browbeats everyone else. This person leaves meetings frustrated and angry because he doesn't get what he wants from the people who work for him. He never will. It is important to him that he does not. If he did, he would have to review his own actions rather than find fault with others. Focusing outward

Life Prescription

helps him to avoid any feelings about his own inadequacy. This pattern will not stop until he eliminates what is bothering him.

From this viewpoint, people's actions make sense. Their actions eliminate stressful issues, and if people can make their actions work with others, they form patterns that last a lifetime. The purpose of patterns is to specifically and consistently solve our problems. *Patterns are the outcome of problem-solving.*

We develop patterns to give us a systematic way of dealing with events in our world. Each event in our life creates an opportunity for learning. We observe events that occur consistently and create actions to take control, avoid, or embrace those events when they occur again. In other words, patterns are used to "make sense" out of the events surrounding us as we grow up.

A young boy I knew had been abused by his mother. She did not want him to get out of bed after lights out. To keep him in bed she told him that there were "monsters" in the house that would hurt him if he got up. She would wait until he was almost asleep, slip into the room, pull the covers over his head and hit him through the covers. Then she would run away before he could see who it was. She would tell him that it was the "monsters." She did this consistently when he was a young child. Fortunately, he was taken away from her. When I met him, he had problem-solved the "monsters." He would sing a song he had made up to appease the "monsters" every night when he went to sleep. He did it in a very ritualized way. And, wouldn't you know it, since he had been away from his mother, the song worked. He was very pleased he had found a way to control the "monsters," and would not accept any other explanation for their disappearance.

Expecting Others to Participate in Our Patterns

A pattern makes sense to its owner. Once you develop a pattern that works for you, you believe that everyone you meet will be a participant in it. In the early 1980s, I was a partner in owning a sailboat with a fellow who was an excellent sailor. I was not. One blustery October day, he wanted to take the boat out. I was convinced that it was too windy. He persuaded me to go with him and his two sons. Half-way into Big Creek on Lake Lanier, he let his older son take the tiller. I was not worried because we had the jib down and the mainsail reefed, which greatly reduced our speed. Suddenly, my partner jumped to the front of the boat and pulled up the jib. We continued to do all right until we crossed into the main channel, when the force of the wind immediately tripled. Almost at once, we went over, and everyone fell into water that was well below fifty degrees. Fortunately, a houseboat saw us capsize and came to our rescue. No one was hurt, but after we towed the sailboat into harbor, I asked my friend why he had let his son skipper, and then put up more sail. He responded that he felt that everyone was as good a sailor as he was. It had never entered his mind that he was turning the helm over to an inexperienced sailor. He believed that if he could handle the wind so could everyone else—obviously, untrue.

The same beliefs are true of other patterns. If a person cannot tolerate authority, for example, he will create a systematic rebellion that will justify his actions and reactions to authority. Once it is a successful pattern, the person expects all people in authority to treat him in the same manner as the original authority figure who helped create the pattern. Just as a projector in a movie theater projects the image onto the screen, each of us projects our patterns onto others, wanting them to participate as *we* expect. We make people fit into our patterns by using fantasy or we adjust the pattern so that it makes sense to others as it does to us.

CHAPTER • 5

Patterning Process:
Problems, Orientation, Testing

Basic Problems—The What and the How

As an adult, the experience that made me feel the most helpless and useless came as I stepped off an airplane in Vietnam. I was in a different country, a hostile country, where I did not know how life was lived. No training prepared me for the actions taken in war. The setting was chaotic and the strategy simple. Stay alive. In the beginning, I felt useless because I did not know how actions took place. I could not participate successfully in what was occurring. I was useless until I learned, and learned very quickly, what the rules of the game were. Until then, I was not accepted into the combat group. Unless I could pull my weight and protect the group, the group did not want me. I was a liability that hampered the group goal of survival. Each new soldier traveled the same path, learning how to survive and how to help the group survive—to learn the operating rules of this new and different environment.

Two basic problems are at the root of the patterning process. The first is *What can I do?* What are my capabilities in response to any event I face? Can I finish this book on time? In the work setting, can I ask the right questions? Can I get the job done? When a person faces an upset boss, a busy intersection, or a barking dog, he wants to see if he can successfully exercise *control* over the situation.

Any event that is not understandable can be considered a problem. In fact, *any unexpected problem can be a trauma.* Stressful events occur to everybody. For example, a young mother was obsessed with not allowing her daughter out of her sight. Even as the child matured, the mother's need for control did not diminish. Her daughter, at twenty years old, wanted to cut the cord between the two of them. As the cord frayed, the mother panicked and started demanding greater control. When the daughter wanted to leave home for college, the mother's controlling actions caused a fight.

All her life the child used normal social avenues, such as church and school, to be able to interact with the world. She realized that everybody else's mother did not protect them the same way hers did. The child believed that her mother's actions were ridiculous, and she was absolutely correct. But she had no knowledge of the cause of her mother's actions.

Eventually, the mother revealed that her daughter had been run over by a truck when she was four years old. The mother felt totally responsible because she had left her child in the front yard alone. After her daughter survived this trauma, the mother made a decision to never leave her alone again. When the mother retold the incident of the truck, the child remembered her mother saying over and over through the years how lucky they were, and how she would watch her daughter carefully from this point forward. So a pattern of extreme overprotection evolved.

When a person decides on his solution to a problem, he does not examine that decision anymore. Often, the decision is limited by capacity or information. In other words, you don't know all your op-

Patterning Process: Problems, Orientation, Testing

tions. You don't know all the possibilities when you make the decision, but because it works, you continue to use it over time. At the time of a problem, the *What can I do?* is the range of available options. The range is never static and the options expand as we get older. In our example, the mother made a good choice for the safety of a four-year-old, but the choice wore thin when the daughter was twenty.

The second basic problem is *How can I do it?* This involves picking a strategy that is workable for me in my circumstances, and then trying it out. The strategy I ultimately select is the one that works. When my son was five, he went through a period of being afraid of the dark. To overcome his fear, we tried the standard remedies—night lights, stories about the dark, being tough. Nothing worked very well. Finally, we found that he would stay in bed if he left his most powerful toys in the doorway to his room. He thought that they could ward off any intruders. Many nights, I walked over the Power Rangers to give him his nighttime hug and kiss. We never put the toys in place. He would arrange them exactly as they needed to be. This strategy worked for him until he grew out of the fear.

This is like the story of the man who walked along a busy downtown street blowing a whistle. It was very irritating to his friends, so one of them asked him why he was blowing it. He responded, "It keeps the elephants away." The friend replied, "There are no elephants within a thousand miles of here!" The man countered, "You see, it works." No bad monsters ever came to get my son. You see, it worked.

Orientation of Patterns

We learn actions both by watching other people and by trial and error. The range of actions and reactions we observe in our caretakers alerts us to what is significant in the environment. This teaches children how to protect themselves. How many times do we say, "Look both ways before you cross the street" or "Don't get too close to the stove"? We spend many hours orienting children to the dangers and delights of our world. On the positive side, picture a one-year-old with his first ice cream cone. At this age, though parents may take precau-

Life Prescription

tions, it is entirely acceptable to wear as much as you eat. Parents enjoy watching a child struggle with his first cone. But what of the eight-year-old? We expect him to know how to eat without spilling, and hold him responsible for this learning.

The orienting process tells the child how adults succeed with ice cream, rainy days, long lines, lost keys, and other encounters with the environment. We want children to succeed, as we do. When they do not, we offer encouragement, scold, or punish. We do so in an attempt to orient the child so that he can behave in an acceptable range—acceptable to us, to the people around us, and to the environment in which we operate. When children show the control we want, we feel we are doing a good job as parents.

This orientation equals the range of skills we bring to the job of parenting. None of us took a special course that prepared us for parenting. No book has the answers, but if we recognize that we are orienting our children toward what they need to know about our environment, the job makes more sense. The better the orientation, the more effective the patterns will be that follow.

But this is no simple stimulus-response process; instead it is a systematic approach that sees the child as a problem-solver. A parent orients his child as to which problems must be solved, and then the child puts this orientation into an effective life pattern.

In the learning process, children face many events they cannot control or understand. Parents know these events. They know the ones that will be painful and the ones that will be pleasurable. Parents are guides into an unknown world for the child. For his part, the child will problem-solve the world quickly. What parent has not marveled at the skill of communication mastered by preverbal children? Mothers will tell you that different cries mean different things—from "come change me" to "I'm hurt." I saw a one-year-old at an adult party go up to her mother and flash her by raising her dress overhead. The mother was embarrassed and sent her away. The child then went to her father and repeated the action. He, too, pulled her dress back down, and laughed it off. This action continued for twenty minutes with the child going first to one, then the other of her parents. Finally, she went to several strangers. One of the older mothers took one look at her and said to the mother, "She's wet, you should check her." The child knew what had to happen to get changed, even if the parents ignored her communications. This little girl was testing the patterns her parents had given her. Testing is the second element of learning patterns.

Using Controls and Testing

In this example, the little girl at the party problem-solved "getting changed" the best she knew how, by raising her dress and waiting to be checked by someone who could do something about it. But this test was not understood by her parents, who had oriented her about "getting changed."

Parents often miss tests because they do not think of children as problem-solvers who are going to test them. An eight-year-old screams, "I hate you!" This is a wonderful test for any parent. If children know this test, they will use it when an adult gets too close to a problem. They use this test to push the adult away and then they wait to see if the adult becomes more controllable. One response to this test is, "You don't know me well enough to hate me. Wait until you grow up and know me a little better; then you can decide if you want to hate me or not." Children are usually surprised by this response. Predictably, what would be an adult's response if a small child screamed "I hate you"? Probably, "No, you shouldn't say that!" Adults get upset—yet not getting upset offers an opening for the child to examine whether his test is working.

Sometimes kids reveal horrible information about themselves early in a relationship. They think this will revolt most adults. Their goal is to test adult reactions. They learn how to push adults away and control the situation. Even though they would like an adult to come closer, it is safer to push him away and keep control.

All patterns go back to the two original problems: *What can I do?* (i.e., what type of control do I have?), and *How can I do it?* (i.e., what can I do that I can predict will offer me success?). When I throw an action at you, I want to be able to predict what you will do. If I don't get the reaction I expect, then I don't have control, and I must create another test.

To summarize, the patterning process evolves as follows:

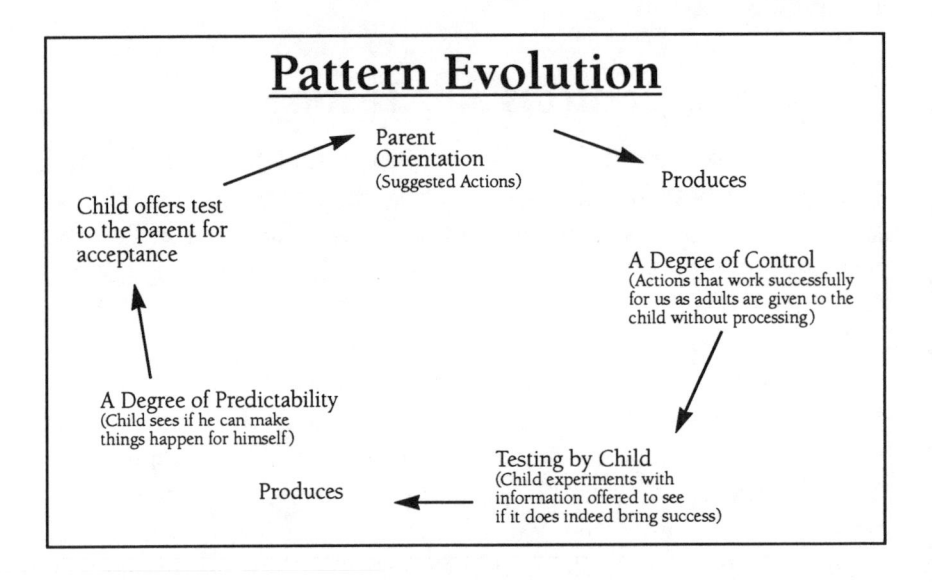

Pattern Evolution

Child offers test to the parent for acceptance

→ Parent Orientation (Suggested Actions)

Produces →

A Degree of Control (Actions that work successfully for us as adults are given to the child without processing)

↓

Testing by Child (Child experiments with information offered to see if it does indeed bring success)

← Produces

A Degree of Predictability (Child sees if he can make things happen for himself)

↑

CHAPTER • 6

Patterning Process:
Learning from Adult Patterns

The Effect of Parents' Problem-Solving on Children

A parent's actions become problems that her child problem-solves. Parental actions can hurt or help a child as he struggles to negotiate the changes from other-control to self-control and dependence to independence. During this struggle, the parent teaches her child what she knows about problem-solving the world. When the mother learned problem-solving, it was in response to a real or perceived need. For example, during the depression, food was scarce. People had to be very careful about how they handled their supplies. Children learned by the actions of adults to deny themselves luxuries and to survive on minimal amounts of food. Later in life, many of these grown-up children remained frugal and avoided wasting food, even though the depression was over.

What parents teach is a product of the events going on in the environment and the way their own parents approached problem-solving. The style of problem-solving parents use is the one they understand best. That style may fit the circumstances or it may not. Often, circumstances will change, only to have the problem-solving strategy remain the same.

Let's look at problem-solving styles—when they are used and how.

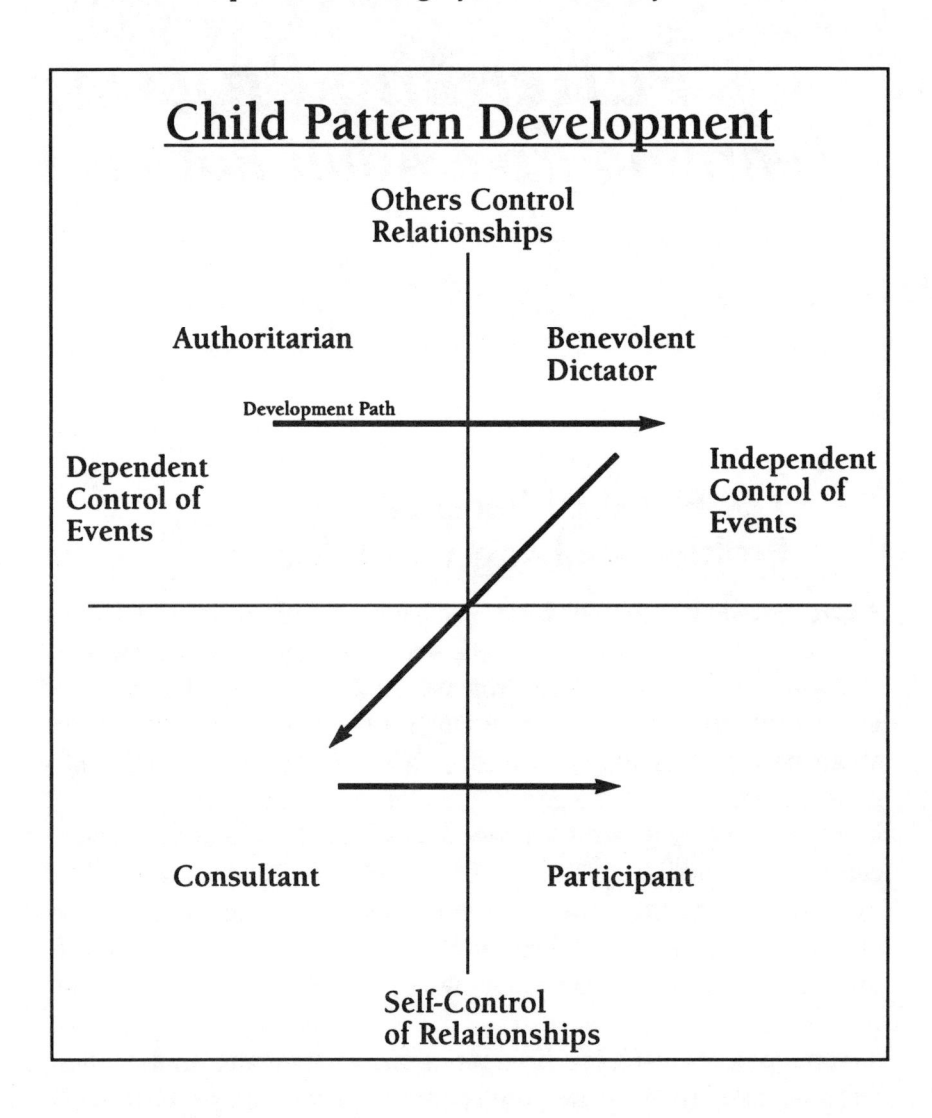

Child Pattern Development

Others Control Relationships

Authoritarian | Benevolent Dictator

Development Path →

Dependent Control of Events | Independent Control of Events

Consultant | Participant

Self-Control of Relationships

Each of the quadrants has one combination of attributes. For example, the upper-left quadrant is *other-control* and *dependence*. Obviously, a person in this state would need a strong hand to guide him, someone using the authoritarian style of problem-solving.

The Authoritarian

By definition, an authority has the power to give commands, enforce obedience, take action, and make final decisions. Obviously, this type of problem-solving is heavily controlling. This style is natural when caring for an infant. No infant can care for herself. The events that occur in her life are all out of her control. A wet diaper, a door slamming, and feeding time are all out of her control. Someone must take definite action to ensure her well-being.

An authoritarian person makes strong calls. He does not waver on decisions. Issues are distinctly black and white. This style of "tell the other what to do" is exactly what a child new to the world needs. He needs a strong hand to keep him out of harm's way and to introduce firm boundaries about what is right and wrong. This period of life is the "hot stove time," when children want to touch and taste things that will hurt them. A strong person must say "No" and make it stick. Notice that the style and the learning needs of the child fit together. The child is dependent and does not understand the world. The parent takes a strong stand and holds consistently to what is "Yes" and "No." With this clear direction, a safe and secure child emerges, prepared to explore acceptable areas and ready to avoid dangers.

This is normal care for a young child. A parent senses what the child needs and takes care of those needs. This action is appropriate to the needs of the child. It is a healthy use of authority.

Authority becomes unhealthy when, after children grow up, adults continue telling them exactly what to do and how to do it without giving them any independence or self-control. Bosses often behave this way in the workplace. They assume total control, and employees must wait on them to decide everything. The boss then becomes angry because no one takes any initiative. An unhealthy authoritarian is a total dictator.

In our present society, one often thinks of authority as only negative. It doesn't have to be. When you walk into a system that is chaotic, where people don't feel a lot of self-control or independence, very often the most effective leader solves the chaos by telling people exactly what they are going to do and how they are going to do it—at first. A positive authoritarian is very strong and guiding. She makes good, concise decisions and sticks to them. A positive authoritarian takes control and orders the situation. She solves the problem of getting a project started. But as people learn their task better and feel more self-control and independence, the authoritarian problem-solver moves into a different style.

The Benevolent Dictator

A benevolent dictator problem-solving style combines a person who wishes well and one with supreme authority appointed in times of emergency. In the upper-right quadrant, the child has more control over events in his world than self-control. He will act impulsively, touch anything that crosses his path—a path that is very often outside his parent's view. Only later does the parent learn about the child's transgressions. If you notice, as you move into this quadrant, you still are under other people's control. There are still a lot of things a child doesn't know about—rattlesnakes, roads, cabinets, poisons. She is still impulsive about running into the street. She doesn't understand the full danger of the world. At the same time, she has quick little feet and graspy hands. She has great energy and curiosity. What is mommy's hair gel all about? How do I get the door open? What does this taste like? She does not know about boundaries. She sees older siblings and parents make things work for them so she tests them out—not fully knowing what will happen.

In the same vein, parents want a child to feed and dress herself, to go to the bathroom independently. Even though they must hold authority, good parents recognize, accept, and expect some independence. They are simply trying to ensure that a child's independence does not cross the lines of safety or impropriety.

Not wanting to restrict their child too much, parents allow some self-orientating to occur. When the child gets beyond acceptable boundaries, the parent dictates a stop to her actions and may or may not punish her. When punishment occurs, the parent reduces independent action, forcing the child back into the dependent area of our diagram. The desired outcome is for the child to learn appropriate actions for each environment. For example, children may yell and whoop all they want on the playground, but must sit still and listen in church or the classroom.

Even benevolent dictators may exhibit other styles of problem-solving, depending on their own patterns. For example, if a parent has a pattern that is a phobia of dogs, he may not allow his child to be around dogs, not even puppies. Such a parent may set clear boundaries, but rather than allow the child to test and understand them, as he does as a benevolent dictator, he reverts and becomes an authoritarian in the areas that he can not tolerate personally.

A second problem arises when parents are too loose in the boundaries they set. They ignore certain actions that require a response. As a result, children cannot find consistency to the parents' actions and are unsure how to behave, often testing with less and less acceptable behavior.

As children grow older, they find new environments to conquer. The rules shift again. Once children are capable of producing the appropriate response for each environment, parents begin a new type of problem-solving.

The Consultant

A consultant is someone who gives advice or instruction. No longer having to contain or control a child's actions, the parent can help her test her problem-solving. As the child learns to function in multiple situations, such as school, church, and work, the parent acts as a consultant. This commonly occurs when a child falls in love for the first time or goes for the first job interview. Parents have experienced these events themselves and can offer advice about how to succeed.

What happens when you try a new activity? Let's suppose you go canoeing with your child. Certain actions require cold authority while canoeing. Forceful reminders are required to ensure a safe and comfortable trip. But after fifteen or twenty canoe trips, a child may have enough skill to allow the parent to assume a consulting role.

Suppose you are canoeing with your son on a river you have traveled many times. The weather is hot. Your son wants to remove his life jacket. The water is only a foot and a half deep. You advise him to keep the jacket on. If he pushes you to take it off, you may have to resort to being a benevolent dictator or an authoritarian. To do that, you may have to stop the canoe. By this action, you say to the child, "You are now dependent on me and have no control over this event until you take the action I require, which is putting the life jacket back on."

Another example is brushing teeth. A parent brushes his daughter's teeth, but he wants her to brush on her own. As a benevolent dictator, he continues to maintain limits so that the child will adopt this habit. Later, he may be a consultant, offering advice on the sources of bad breath and the effect of yellow teeth on one's social life in an effort to keep brushing a habit. Medication is another good example. Suppose you want your child to take some medicine—an antibiotic or seizure medication, for example. She starts playing with you, controlling whether she swallows it. As a consultant, you have to persuade her to take the medicine.

As soon as they have some self-control, children latch on to the *"not have to's"*—things that their parents told them they have to do, but they don't *really* have to. Such activities as brushing teeth and eating breakfast are things parents tout as important, but children may think they "don't have to." Differing information presents itself to the child. Parents help their children to sort it out.

For a parent, unhealthy consulting means giving bad advice or no advice when it is needed. Suppose I never faced bullies growing up and I never got into a fight. I was always a good kid. I won't have any advice to give when my child brings me a bully problem. Quite possibly, I might avoid the subject. Or, for example, a parent takes a child to the dentist, knowing that she has to have two teeth pulled. A good consulting parent prepares the child for what's coming by telling her what is going to happen, how it is going to happen, and what the dentist is going to do. This allows a child to be mentally prepared. If the event occurs as described, she will be more comfortable and accepting of the procedure, no matter how unpleasant.

Recently I was told of a young boy who needed stitches. An adult he trusted explained stitches to him and tugged the skin on his arm to show him what it would feel like. The parent was present, but had never had stitches and could not give any examples that would ease the boy's worry. Soon after the demonstration, the boy relaxed and was calm when he got the stitches.

When a consultant gives valued advice, he becomes valuable. Do you want to lose your job as a consultant and have to fight with your kids all the time about their actions? All you need to do is give them advice on topics about which you know nothing. A better option is to talk to them about the issues and help them to arrive at their own ideas. When the ideas work, your consulting value rises.

What if you make a mistake and give wrong advice? Most mistakes can be fixed—as long as there is a relationship. You can have a bad day and, perhaps, feeling under pressure from your boss, you slip into an authoritarian style at the wrong time. You can fix it. Just say, "I'm sorry. I was wrong. I made a mistake." Admitting a mistake is the behavior of a consultant. It's the right thing to do in this situation, rather than behaving like an authoritarian or benevolent dictator and refusing to admit your mistake.

After you have made a mistake is the best time to reflect and change your action. When a feeling is too strong to problem-solve during the event, you can correct it before the next event. Discuss it between events. Working to correct a problem is what makes us problem-solvers. By determining what doesn't work very well, you learn what you can do about it.

The Participant

A participative problem-solving style is used by someone who takes part and shares with others. In the lower-right quadrant of the diagram (see page 30), the parent's training job is mostly done. Children

Life Prescription

have the skills to succeed. Later, as adults, children may revisit any of the positions in the diagram, depending on what circumstances they find in their life. They may ask a parent to consult or they may need a parent to order them back within solid boundaries. From time to time, they may need a kick in the pants.

In the last quadrant, it is the child who asks the parent to participate in his life events. The relationship between the two is mature, with a respect for decisions and boundaries. Children in this quadrant are fully capable of making good, sensible decisions, and parents and children experience events together. For example, suppose a young man gets dumped by a girlfriend or his friend is killed in an automobile accident. A parent does not have to give advice, but simply recognize and share the experience—just as one would do with any other normal adult.

When does problem-solving become participative? The answer is when a child knows most of the events she will face and makes good decisions about them. You may be a consultant until your children leave home, or you may find that a bright, well-behaved child allows you to become participative while she is still in high school, or even before. As a parent, there will be times when you will be participative with young children, but young children do not know when to quit—they do not understand the limits like older children do. My son likes to wrestle, but if I do not set a time limit, he gets excited and cannot stop.

Sharing in relationships doesn't mean going along on your children's dates, but it does mean, if your relationship is strong, that they want to tell you what's happening in their lives. You listen and support. For example, a father called to check on a job interview. He listened to his daughter's experience and responded, "Well, it sounds like you are doing it exactly right." He did not consult, only listened.

Knowing When to Use Which Problem-Solving Style

If a parent teaches a child the appropriate times to be an authoritarian, a benevolent dictator, a consultant, and a participant, the child gains a full, healthy, flexible range of problem-solving skills. Unfortunately, not all of us had parents who used the whole range with us. For example, a father and son work on projects together, but the father is a perfectionist. The son is too young to be of any real help on the project. The father becomes frustrated and yells at the boy. The child runs from his father in fear and shame. The father feels awful, knowing that he hurt his son. When we review the father's problem-solving style during these projects, we find that he is uncomfortable. He does not feel confident. In his childhood, he was unable to work with his father. So, even though the father has immense patience with his son in other circumstances, he has no pattern that allows him to work successfully with his son on projects.

In another example, a normally calm person becomes extremely ill-tempered with his family while packing for vacations. In review, this person always saw his mother act the same way when her family went on vacations. When he was a child, vacations needed a fight to get started. Recognizing what quadrant a child is operating in is half the battle. Watching to see what problem-solving style you use is the rest.

Integrated Problem-Solving

The last point about problem-solving styles is the importance of an integrated approach. Integrated problem-solving means that any problem has two components—a situation and a relationship—and they affect the solution. If a child walks up to a rattlesnake, you are not going to be participative or consultative. You are going to be authoritarian. If a child wants to know what dress to wear to the prom, you are probably going to be a consultant unless it is an inappropriate dress, and then you may have to become authoritarian. The skill is being able to use any one of these styles without damaging the relationship or your child's independence.

A parent may assume any role in the diagram during a child's life. By the way their parents *act* when they use these problem-solving styles, children learn how to use them also. This teaching of styles is critical to the child's success in learning about how to get along in the world. When parents are limited in the problem-solving styles they use and the situations in which they use them, children have less of an opportunity to learn appropriate styles.

Suppose a child only learned the authoritarian style while growing up. Once she accepted this as the proper way to negotiate the world, she would not question her own thoughts or decisions. The first time a teacher directed her to do something, she might rebel because following others' rules would not be a familiar problem-solving response. Or a child who only understood the authoritarian style might have a field day manipulating an adult who sought to deal with her using the participative style.

The strongest and healthiest personalities are able to use all problem-solving styles. This flexibility allows adults to work with a wide range of people without feeling any loss of control, either from relationships or events in their environment. They are able to quickly adjust and adapt to changes and not lose perspective.

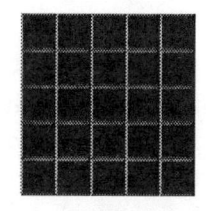

CHAPTER • 7

Patterning Process: Rules

Three basic rules govern pattern formation: people gravitate to their greatest acceptance, nothing is random, and nothing happens in isolation.

People gravitate to their greatest acceptance. When people are problem-solving, gathering information, and testing their patterns, they will stick with the actions that are most acceptable over time. Did you ever wonder about children being under a bad influence? Or, why your teenager is more interested in being with the guys than being with the family? What about when your spouse insists on a weekly outing with office friends? People gravitate to others who accept them. Over time, they want interactions with these people rather than with those who are critical or abrasive.

This does not mean that people will not problem-solve a pattern around an abusive boss. On the contrary, they find ingenious ways of avoiding the wrath of the boss. They problem-solve by withholding information that will be used on themselves or others later. This protective process may be the simple act of not inviting the boss to meetings. It may involve the collusion of co-workers. One bright office manager, who had a standing meeting with her abusive boss, moved it to a time and day when the boss only had one hour before he had to attend another meeting, which effectively limited the length of their interaction. She made a list of all major topics, separated it into critical and noncritical topics, and only brought up the noncritical ones with him. In this way, he never had enough information to attack her work.

In their jobs, people respond to warmth and help. In the long run, they will form relationships with accepting people while they problem-solve and stymie a tyrant.

Nothing is random. Even though it may appear that random activity is taking place, the actions are designed to bring success to the person performing them. If actions were random, the outcome would be arbitrary. No one could produce a pattern. No controls would evolve, interactions would be chaotic, and social structure nonexistent. When people problem-solve, we work the randomness out of our solution. We test to produce consistency of results. After all, we are going to use this information for the rest of our lives, so shouldn't we be sure that it works specifically and consistently?

Nothing happens in isolation. Isolation is where people go to avoid interaction. In isolation, there are no opportunities to receive new information or to change. In isolation, people are able to hold on to a belief because there are no challenges to it. In isolation, the only person we test is ourselves.

In the late seventies, a social worker found a child locked in a single room of a house. The child had spent most of his life locked in that dark room. The only light came in under the door. Food was passed through the same crack. No training or hygiene was taught and the child did whatever he chose to pass the time. The child had never attended school and had no playmates except house mice. He was never allowed out of the room.

When he was discovered by the social worker at the age of ten, he could make sounds, but not talk. He did not walk upright. He had excellent night vision, but was extremely sensitive to light. His hearing was very acute, and his movement on all fours quick and dexterous. One might think that if you took this child out of the isolated situation, he would begin to learn and eventually grow properly. This was not the case, however, because of his patterns. He had problem-solved being in that room for ten years. He was very good at it. His senses were adapted to the input given to him. He had successful isolation patterns.

The same was true of prisoners in Nazi concentration camps during World War II. When they were released and told they could leave the camps, many were slow to do so. It was difficult for them to conceive of leaving the enclosed area that had been home for so many years. They had adapted to the pattern of isolation. Sadly, such isolation is so intense that it colors all later attempts to change, holding a person in its grip because of its fearful intensity.

The reality is that nothing happens and nothing changes in isolation. I can't get rid of my feelings by isolating myself. I can cause them to diminish by avoiding events, which gives me a false sense of control. The next time I come into contact with the same people, I am going to end up with the same set of feelings. So, I either have to avoid interaction altogether or I have to cope with those feelings. In other words, if I isolate myself, I can control the situation and I can control my feelings, but I have only solved the problem temporarily.

Have you ever been in contact with somebody you really didn't like? Think about how you can control your feelings as long as you are away from that person, but when you walk into a room and encounter that person you get an aversive feeling. You don't know how to respond to eliminate that feeling. You know that by isolating yourself, however, you can control it. This greater control relieves feelings of discomfort. But although pulling back might make you feel better, it doesn't change anything.

Test anxiety is the same thing, and so is speaking phobia. We can isolate ourselves from any occurrence, and cope pretty well. Suppose you have a phobia of cats. You stay in your apartment where there are no pets allowed. You stay in your car. As long as you isolate yourself, you are fine. But if you ever get out, walk the neighborhood or

Life Prescription

go to a friend's house, you may find a cat. Then the feeling rushes back, and you don't have a responsible coping method.

Understanding and admitting how we push people to fit our patterns is key to understanding how patterns work. If I expect you to be bad to me, then I'm going to force you to be bad so you will fit my pattern.

A friend told me he had visited his nephew in Atlanta. When he was packing his car to leave, the nephew kept coming up and asking ten thousand questions. My friend needed to make a decision about how to handle the situation. What he said was, "Henry, quit bugging me. Go do something."

The nephew had been adopted from a troubled family. He always expected someone to leave him. The boy manipulated the situation by asking inane questions until his uncle pushed him away. "Go away" is not that far from "run away." Since both individuals were acting out an unhealthy pattern, I asked my friend, "Who won?" "Nobody won," was the reply. But, in reality, both won because both got what they wanted. The uncle got to escape Henry, because he was getting on his nerves. Henry got to be pushed away.

To replace an unhealthy action with a healthy action, the uncle could have said, "Henry, I like you a lot, but I'm busy right now and have to leave. Can we do something later?" A reaction of support and acceptance is all that is required. The simplest answer is normally the best.

Regarding the rules of the patterning process, remember *event, feeling, decision, responsibility, elimination*. What will your decision be and what is your responsibility to any given event or feeling? If, as a child, you solve a problem by exploding angrily and force people to react your way then, as an adult, you also will become explosive and force people to deal with your anger. The same thinking applies in an older setting.

When a person is young, he chooses an action. For him, the action works. The action is accepted or ignored by others. The acceptance or rejection supports the solution. This solution is not random, but is specific to the user. It does not happen in isolation. It works to reduce tension in the life of the user. Over a period of time, it becomes a pattern. When a person becomes an adult, he is basically doing the same thing that he learned to do when he was five years old.

A young friend of mine said, "At twenty-eight years old, I realize that I keep doing things over and over that I think don't make sense. What you are saying is that they really do make sense, because that's how I problem-solved my life. I have to look at the way I've learned to problem-solve. Those methods made sense to a three-year-old child, but not to me at twenty-eight years old." The circumstances may have changed, but the course of the river has not changed.

We have to overcome our resistance to change by understanding what our patterns are and then saying, and truly meaning, "I don't want this to be in my life anymore." Once we have seriously made this decision, we must act upon it. And we must work through the anxiety associated with this shift in action *by acting*. No one works it through just by thinking. You can think about it until your brain shrinks. But you will not make a change until you act.

In another example, a fellow (let's call him Tom) felt extremely powerless. Tom's dad was abusive. His mom babied him. He learned to problem-solve not by being confrontational, but by being nice, being everybody's buddy. At the same time, he resented this "nice guy" action, because when he was nice, Tom felt he had no power. He felt that his niceness gave power to others around him. To be happy at all, Tom learned to take control of his life in a passive way. His passivity created isolation, but by avoiding conflict he also could not acquire new information. Tom gravitated to powerful people even though he was uncomfortable with them. His actions were not random, but grew out of fear of his father, and the support, without real relief, of his mother.

To look for patterns in this example, we must ask several questions. The first is, what does Tom want? As a young child, he claimed to not know what he wanted. What he wanted was "something," but it was random. Tom did not know why he felt angry and rebellious against authority. He didn't understand why he resented it when people told him what to do. He didn't understand why he felt resentment toward his mom when she was nice to him. When Tom got older, he realized that he thought his mother was doing the same thing that he was doing. By being nice to him, she was trying to get something out of him. Manipulation became his problem-solving method. Once he developed his pattern, he had to believe that every person was more powerful than himself. As he engaged these people, he expected them to overpower him as his father had. He thought that the only way to keep any control in his life was to be passive and manipulative. In this pattern, he expected all people in authority to treat him the way the person who originally caused the problem treated him. To react in a different way from what originally worked with his father would not work now. Tom's solution was to become passive with aggressive people, but he resented it and manipulated them whenever he could.

A singular question remains: did his father really treat him that way or was that only Tom's perception? I'm sure Tom's parents didn't mean for him to have to go around feeling overpowered, but the problem occurred when he was so young he didn't understand how to confront it in a healthy way, by telling his parents he felt out of control and didn't like it. In pattern formation, it doesn't matter whether the event is real or imagined. The reality is that it becomes an event in this person's life, creating a feeling that he wants to release. The passive, angry mechanism he uses to release it is the only response action he can muster at the time. The angry, passive mechanism works because he can withdraw enough from the power, be angry enough at the power, and make himself feel as if he is not helpless against the power.

Later in his life, Tom's solution caused difficulty with principals and bosses, but he could still perform because he became passive rather than exploding at the authority. If he had exploded in certain situations, those in authority would have been justified in controlling him. But since he pulled away and became passive, he found an acceptable, though uncomfortable, way to control the authority.

What did Tom get from this pattern? First, he got to be liked, as he developed an outgoing, social way of interacting. At an early age, he realized that if he made people like him, he could get what he wanted. When people made him angry, he did not confront them, but placated them to get what he wanted. Second, to keep the pattern operating, he needed people who, he thought, had control over him. To support his solution, Tom gave his power to other people. He exposed facts about himself. He gave others more knowledge about him than they needed. When they used that knowledge against him, he was justified in feeling that they were more powerful.

With Tom, everything evolved around control. As a child, he was helpless and dependent. How did he work out of that normal childhood situation? What can you become and what can you make of the world as a growing, bright, adapting being? *What can you do? How can you do it?* Everyone is trying to respond to those two questions, and ultimately, Tom's patterns answered them.

Once the questions are resolved, why would anybody ever want to change their solution? The only reason pattern solutions change is when they do not work. In moving a successful pattern from a family unit of two or three people to a church unit or community unit, the pattern may reach a point where it doesn't accomplish the things that it accomplished in a smaller environment. What most people do is apply the rules. How can they generate their greatest acceptance? How can they work out non-random, specific solutions? How can they avoid the pain of isolation, and stay active in the group? *A person can either adjust his pattern to make it work in other environments or develop a new pattern.*

CHAPTER • 8

Pattern Operation

One major difference separates children's pattern building from adult pattern operation. During childhood, a child is problem-solving the events in his world. As an adult, the solutions are in place. Decisions have been made and are expected to bring results. Adults rarely retrace their problem-solving process. They are satisfied with the results, even if only marginally.

For example, the head of a major company was under stress at home. He would come to the office and explode at the people who worked for him. His employees expected this behavior from time to time, but it started to become excessive. The normal reaction to someone who explodes is to get out of his way. So at work, people stopped bringing problems to this explosive person. They started handling these problems on their own, solving them to the best of their ability, and refusing to involve the boss. Over time, what happened? Pressure on the explosive person subsided. He got exactly what he was working for—to keep people from bothering him!

If one studies the *event, feeling, decision, responsibility, elimination* process in connection with this example, its exact history is not in doubt. Somewhere in his background this person learned that, when

Life Prescription

he is under stress, exploding at other people deflects additional responsibility.

Perhaps when he was a five-year-old, his parents wanted him to eat supper. He screamed and threw a tantrum, and all of a sudden they said, "O.K., forget it!" Or he watched his dad scream at his mom, and Mom backed off. Actions are learned. At some point in his early life, he was oriented to this action, tested it, and got it to work for him. Because it worked, he used it consistently.

Often, people think of their lives as a series of snapshots. We remember significant events such as weddings, a baby's birth, or the big game. In reality, our lives are like a motion picture, frame after frame moving forward. The key events we remember are important because they occurred close enough to us to affect our emotions.

I was in a hypnosis review class several years ago. The instructor had us pick our favorite place to visit, and visit it under hypnosis. Immediately, I chose my family's summer cabin on Lake Lanier, outside of Atlanta. This place had many strong memories for me. It was a small, fifty-foot trailer perched above the lake with a screened porch across the front. The view was spectacular. On a clear day, I thought I could see several miles across the lake. I particularly remember that I could drive up the huge hill to the cabin and feel layers of tension lift off my shoulders as I got out of the car. Even in graduate school, I refused to work in a study group. Instead, I went to the cabin and in that relaxed atmosphere prepared for my written exams.

Under hypnosis, the instructor told us to remember the sights, sounds, and smells surrounding this special place. I thought that I knew every aspect of the experience, but I found that as I retraced my actions to enter the cabin, I learned something. The beginning to my cabin relaxation was a sound. When I got the key from under the tongue of the trailer, I would flip the lock over to open it. The sound of the lock—click-clack—against the screened door was the invitation to begin relaxing. I had never made the association before that class.

Patterns have these components: *events, feelings, decisions, responsibilities, and elimination.* An event causes comfort or discomfort. To

Pattern Operation

relieve discomfort, you make a decision and it works. You produce an action based on your decision. You are able to produce a response, such as a tantrum. You find that after the tantrum you don't have to eat your spinach. You get what you want. So, when you grow up and someone challenges you at work and you feel that unease, the old explosion takes place on an adult level. The other person goes off muttering under his breath, but you end up not having to write the report that he wants you to write. It works. You may say that you didn't really mean to treat that person that way, but the sense of relief that you create for yourself because the pattern worked is stronger than the remorse you feel for having made somebody angry.

You expect your pattern to work. Once you've adapted it and you have it under control, you expect it to produce a predictable outcome between yourself and other people. You expect it to win something for you. It reduces the tension of the event or the feeling. Because it works, it becomes a standard for action that you apply to a whole range of different environments. It applies to work, to school, and to church.

Suppose you are a hot-shot on a small-town football team. As the star player, you are drafted by the University of Georgia or another big school. You are now expected to compete with people whose skill is the same or better than yours. What may have been a good performance for a high school football player may not measure up for a college player. You have to continue to improve your skills and change your patterns, making adjustments based on new demands. Otherwise, an internal conflict arises: "I was really a good high school football player, but I'm no good now that I am in college." Look at Doug Fluty. He was great in college, but he is only five feet, ten inches tall. In the pros, he can't see over the average lineman, who is anywhere from six feet, six inches to six feet, eight inches tall. When he drops back to pass and his field of vision is blocked because of a change in the environment, he faces a conflict. Can he play in the pro arena or not? His height is well-known. Every other team will defend him using this knowledge. He will have to adjust his style of play by rethinking the specifics, consistency, and control that his previous play offered.

Life Prescription

The team he plays for may need to adjust also. If the team intends to compete in the championship, it has a problem. Its pattern of doing things with its old quarterback is not going to work with this quarterback. So the players have to change and be consistent in that change: "We have to block for this new guy every single time. We can't let people through to him or we won't win." Or, in terms of pattern adjustment: "We have to guard him this particular way. We must adjust our play operation to accommodate this problem." The team must become specific about what it can and cannot do—adjust the pattern to effect success in a different environment.

Team members must all be supportive of the adjustments. They all have to change their pattern to make it happen. The issue becomes whether to grouse about having to change a pattern or to see it as a problem to be solved, working with it because these are the given parameters.

Another example of this can be seen in the story of a pilot who was shot down in World War II. He parachuted into the desert. About the third or fourth day without water, he knew he was going to die. All he had was a survival knife and some string. To keep enough moisture in his body to walk out of the desert, he took his survival knife and nicked a vein in his arm, sucking his own blood. It may sound impossible to us, but because he was willing to look at the parameters and say, "This is the only way I will live," he was able to survive the desert. If he had not been willing to examine all of the options, if he had rejected ingesting his blood as a possibility, he would have died.

Once patterned expectations conflict with actual events, a choice must be made. Conflict leads people to accept or reject the possibility of change. Power is in decision. Our pilot said, "How do I survive? I must have water. I can get enough moisture from my blood." If he had rejected this idea, he would have died, but the choice would still have been his.

Some people's learned patterns are more susceptible to change than those of other people. Parents with a pattern of getting excited under tension react impulsively, ignoring many options. Because they im-

Pattern Operation

mediately make a decision for response and elimination when tension arises, they rarely face self-examination. In other words, they pass through problem-solving so fast that they don't take time to stop and make sense of it. I believe this reaction is the problem with learning-disordered children.

Children who are diagnosed with learning disorders are normally bright. They have one deficient area such as math or reading where they cannot learn from standard classroom methods. Many of these children can learn if the teacher will use alternative methods, such as oral testing. Because they are bright and sensitive, these children recognize that they are not learning from the way they are being taught, and that they are different from other students. They feel inadequate to meet the teacher's expectations. As a result, learning-disordered kids test to find all kinds of compensatory actions. One compensation is memorization. This works until about the fifth or sixth grade. At that point, the data becomes too complex and massive to remember, and some children learn how to cheat successfully. They find a buddy who will keep them abreast of what is going on. They may become the class clown so they will be removed from the classroom. Removal works—they cannot be embarrassed by failure if they are not in the class. In most situations, these children never stop to make a decision to get help. They just adapt instead of saying to anyone who would listen, "I need help with this." When the student acts up, teachers may not recognize this behavior as a way to avoid the event (failure at school). The student ends up with a successful event avoidance pattern.

Unless that pattern is broken, it will never change. A psychologist friend of mine did some research on behavior-disordered children in a psychiatric hospital. He found that 34 percent of the children were labeled as behavior-disordered, but were also learning-disordered. He treated them by putting each one in a room with the appropriate-level reading book and telling them to learn how to read the best way they could. He discovered that great variation of styles occurred. Some had to read aloud. Some had to put their finger on every word and go over it three or four times before they grasped the idea. Interestingly, all were able to improve when the pressure was taken off and they were told to "find a way" for themselves. After each found "his way," his behavioral problems decreased.

To understand patterns, one has to follow them to their conclusion. What goal is the pattern trying to produce for the person? Let's suppose you meet an attractive woman. You become involved and cheat on your wife. How does the pattern end? Do you become guilty? Do you end up giving your wife presents? Do you go home and have sex with your wife? *What do you do?* How does the person close the whole pattern? Is the marriage left intact? Because if you are discovered, your relationship can't remain stable. This last statement is true unless your goal is instability in the first place. If instability or hurt is your goal, then you would want your infidelity to come out no matter how painful, so that you could force it beyond an irritation. You could force it into a conflict. The outcome of your actions *is* your goal.

Examples abound: One man was constantly in conflict with bosses. He lost job after job. What was his goal? His goal was to not work for someone else, or simply not to work at all.

Similarly, a child of six used to wait for his mother to come home. He would allow her to get into the house and then would become so rude that she would have to punish him with a spanking. After the spanking and some quiet time in his room, the family would settle down and have a great evening. What was his goal? His goal was to get spanked and be sent to his room.

This goal makes no sense until it is viewed in a larger context. The mother had recently, unexpectedly, divorced. She was angry about the divorce. She had to take a job, something she thought she would never have to do. Her feeling about the *event* was very strong, and she lacked a *decision* to problem-solve the situation. Her son helped her out of the anger by drawing some of it off through his spanking. He became a focus, an easy decision, and part of a pattern to help the mother get along in her new situation. When asked directly, the boy told his mother that he liked the family after he was punished, and felt that his punishment helped the family to get along better.

Pattern Operation

For the parent, the pattern was an easy way to let off some steam. Unless the mother looks at the outcome of this pattern, it may never be recognized for what it is.

In a third case, a teacher was very upset. She could not control her first-grade class. The children spoke out and made noises when she was trying to call on them. When she came to a workshop looking for some help, she started learning how to be specific, consistent, and supportive. She learned how to apply the three rules to her actions. Finally, she understood patterns, and she learned she was a participant in the misbehavior occurring in her classroom. She determined to change her input into the pattern and take control of the classroom. I went for an observation. The students were very well-behaved, happy, and excited about learning. They raised their hands to be called on, and did not grunt to draw attention to themselves. Everyone was called on equally, and they were all learning. She had designed the pattern she wanted to support the goal of self-controlled behavior so that learning could take place, and had implemented it. The children were helping because the pattern made sense to them.

In another setting, I met with a school of primary teachers. They were outraged by the behaviors of the children and wanted something done about it. Before I offered any techniques, I needed to know the goal of the teachers. I asked, "What do you expect the children to do?" They told me. Everything they mentioned was a bad behavior: We expect them to disrupt, be rude, fight, and avoid adult control. I said, "Fine. If you expect them to do that, then their pattern is working exactly the way the kids want it to work." When a teacher expects the same disruption that the child does, the child can control the teacher's reaction. He can predict the way the teacher will come down on him; he prepares for it, and it is not an irritation for him. If a new teacher comes in and the same pattern doesn't work, the kids have to find a new way around the teacher. The environmental parameters are now different. Something has to give. If the teachers only want to complain about children causing disruptions in the classrooms, has it become a serious enough situation that they want to problem-solve it? No. And since it hasn't become serious

Life Prescription

enough to problem-solve, they want to push it off on to a principal, a discipline expert, or alternative school. When it becomes a serious enough irritation—the event, feeling, decision, responsibility—for the teacher to say, "I will now decide how to create the pattern of responses I need to eliminate this process," it will change. When people only complain, they haven't made a decision. A decision is seen in action. All they are doing is expressing a feeling (frustration) about the event with no action. These teachers consider sending a student to the principal's office an action, but it only eliminates the event for a short time and doesn't stop the pattern. When the student comes back, he is going to begin the pattern again. The only way the pattern will stop is if the child makes a different decision, or if the teacher decides to set limits to force a different decision.

A principal cannot change the pattern within the classroom. By the same token, you can't change my pattern. I have to make decisions to change my own pattern. Ultimately, the choice comes back to the owner. People who don't want to make decisions or take responsibility will not like this book.

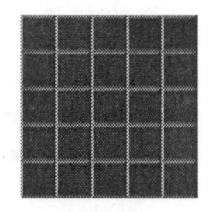

CHAPTER • 9

Pattern Operation and Motivation

What is in it for *me* when it comes to patterns? Patterns work because they produce control and predictability. When other people participate in the patterns with you, you receive support and acceptance for what you do. All patterns lead to this outcome, and are trusted to produce it consistently for you.

Patterns create a process for running your life successfully. You are in control. Control increases your power in interactions and motivates you to compete and continue in these interactions. If you choose patterns that are healthy, the more decisions you make, the more powerful you become. Paradoxically, the more you help other people to become powerful, the more you add to your own power. Eventually, you are surrounded by powerful people. If you are surrounded by powerful people, you are in a position where like-minded powerful people act as a unit, as a group. It all goes back to the patterns.

From a person's actions it is possible to determine what he wants from his pattern. His actions are always a direct reflection of his thinking. In a nutshell, stop listening to what people say and start watching what they do. To learn patterns, you almost have to learn a different type of body language. You have to be able to learn to interpret the language as actions occur.

Actions have a complete process—a complete outcome. Actions are not half-baked. Think about the process of a golf swing. There are a thousand different ways to hit a golf ball. You can hit it with one hand. You can hit it behind your back. But if you want a decent golf shot, you have to follow certain rules. You have to pull the club back, swing through, follow through, turn, keep your head down, etc.

One interesting thing about a golf swing is that if you have a handicap, a temporary leg ache or a hurt back, you are going to compensate in your swing. Your swing will not be the same as a healthy person's, or as your own when you are not hurt.

Compare this concept to learning patterns. Someone who doesn't know anything about golf is just like a baby (helpless and useless) when it comes to golf. The new golfer has no orientation to golf. To gain an orientation he goes to sources. He goes to his friends. He goes to a pro and pays for lessons. He can learn to play golf in a good pattern or a bad pattern. He can learn to play from people who know how to play or he can gather information from once-a-year golfers. He watches golfers' actions to learn how they solve problems that come up during the game. He works through certain problems he encounters when he tries to play. He learns to deal with golfing situations, maybe even the temperament of playing golf. Instead of getting angry, he learns how to keep his temper. He concentrates on the problem and the actions that a good golfer takes.

If he learns from a bad golfer, however, he learns negative things—poor physical actions and perhaps poor temperament on the golf course. For example, let's examine how Phil Mickleson learned to play golf. First, even though he is not normally left-handed, he plays left-handed golf. He learned to hit the golf ball left-handed because his father taught him to play golf, and he stood facing his father. He copied his father's swing exactly, but what he saw was the mirror image of a right-handed golfer. This became his pattern.

We're constantly watching, emulating, and learning from the exact actions we see. What makes it motivational is when we hit the ball.

When we hit it a long way, we are rewarded for the practice. When we hit it consistently, we learn what to do to hit it every time. The success is the reward.

We have seen that the success of a pattern is rewarding to the owner. What happens within the pattern while the problems are being solved? To understand this, we must look at the research on motivation and problem-solving. Research indicates a direct and proportional relationship between the level of motivation and a person's ability to problem-solve. We can think of motivation in this context as tension.

If a person is faced by a mugger, he may experience a whole range of reactions—everything from fainting to fighting. The type of reaction stems from whatever pattern and experiences the person has had with muggers. People react differently, whether the stressful situation is combat, torture, or a bad time in business. The correlation between motivation (tension) and problem-solving ability can be graphically expressed, like this:

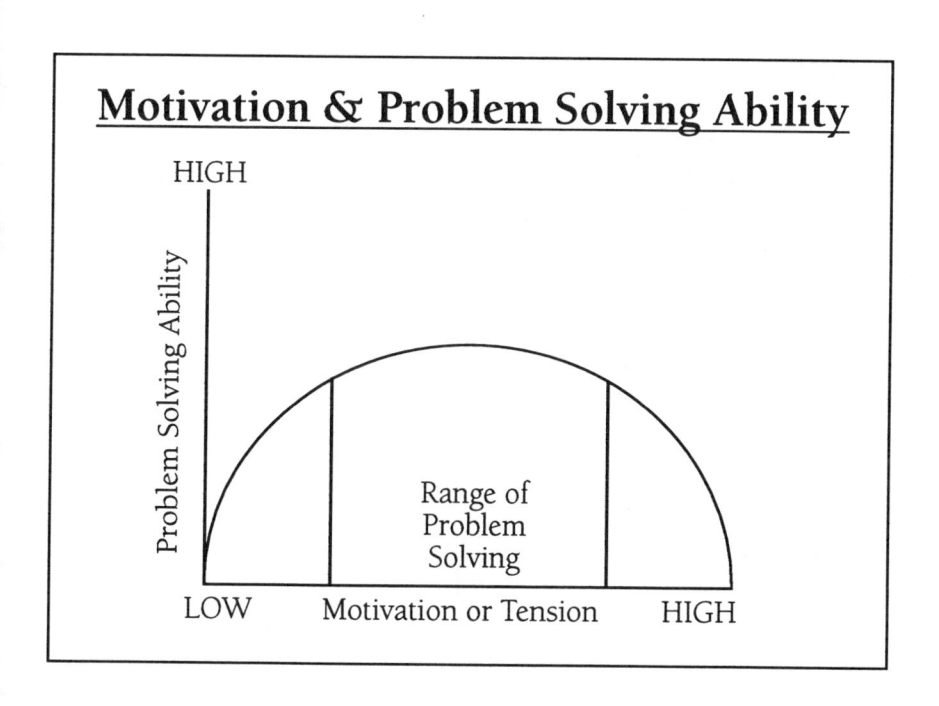

Motivation & Problem Solving Ability

Y-axis: Problem Solving Ability (LOW to HIGH)
X-axis: Motivation or Tension (LOW to HIGH)

Curve shows Range of Problem Solving as an inverted U.

Life Prescription

As discussed earlier, when an event is far enough outside our experience, it does not call for problem-solving. It causes no tension. When an event enters our environment and begins to irritate us, we take a serious stab at problem-solving. But when we have no background orientation—in other words, when we have never tested possible solutions and cannot gather any information about the event—we cannot problem-solve it and the result is massive tension.

In the long haul, tension that cannot be problem-solved causes burnout. Interestingly enough, burnout is a learned response to insoluble problems. If your boss is a tyrant, you can never establish a clear or consistent pattern for handling him. You never know when he may explode at you. You get this anxious feeling in the pit of your stomach on the way to work, but you cannot quit. You've just bought a new house and you need the paycheck. If a feeling seems insoluble, and the event is inescapable, burnout is inevitable. In this last case, the tension may cause you to adapt by creating a safe, emotional depression to avoid some of the pressure.

In pattern formation, tension is necessary to produce problem-solving. If there is too little tension, the problem is not an irritation. Suppose your parents would never let you cross a street. Instead of instructing you about streets, they carried you every time you crossed the street. For you, streets would present no tension because your parents negotiated them. This pattern could occur throughout your life, as your parents negotiated your school, your hairstyle, your friends. You would have few problems to solve because your parents controlled your life successfully. You would be tension-free until you went out on your own. Picking your own friends or your own place to live may then create conflicts with your parents. This is a different motivator—independence. Learning to be on your own and making your own decisions is rewarding. It is part of feeling control within your life.

For years, manufacturing businesses have not allowed independence to be part of the workplace. If a worker wanted to vote, he did it with his feet. The result was the growth of unions. Unions came into the workplace because the conditions provided by management became intolerable. But no matter what the conditions were that led to a union, a major part of the workers' unhappiness involved independence. They wanted to create some specific, consistent, supported pattern for their work lives. The workers problem-solved a lack of independence by forming unions. Today, businesses want teams. Managers who have been trained to keep workers dependent on their decisions are asking workers to form into groups and make decisions about company operation. It certainly sounds like little unions, doesn't it?

In reality, teams could be the positive pattern that businesses should have incorporated before individuals banded together and formed unions. In fact, unionized plants where teams are being formed to enhance the independence of the workers have been very successful. In plants where the teams are an excuse to reduce management cost and pass responsibility to workers, teams are failing miserably.

CHAPTER • 10

Pattern Operation and Dynamic Attractors

In the field of psychology, a dynamic is a force that causes movement. In our lives, we have events and feelings that move us to action. These events and feelings are our dynamics. If I walk across a field wearing a red shirt and a bull comes after me, I am moved to get out of the field. Earlier, I described an experience with lightning. Our whole family felt similarly moved by this event. If I have a bad dream, I can wake up in a sweating terror. If I fall in love with someone, I want to be with her. Both events and feelings are movers for people.

Some events are attractive, like being in love. Some drive us to panic, like nightmares. Once our patterns are formed and are comfortable to us, we move within them. The outcome of our patterns is successful, so we continue to act in the manner we have devised.

In every life come events or feelings that are insoluble. No matter how we try, we cannot make sense of every event and its corresponding feelings. A pre-adolescent recalled the first time someone in his family rebelled about going to church. It is not unusual for older teens to refuse to go to church. But when his sister did, she was harshly disciplined. His reaction, at eleven, was to sit up in bed and cry. Not for his sister, but for the family; he kept asking, "Why do we have to do this?" It did not make sense to him for family members to treat each other that way.

In a similar problem, I remember a parent in a workshop demanding a solution for a child who would not wear shorts. No matter what coercion the parent used, the child refused to wear shorts. My response was that, for his own reasons, her child had decided to wear only long pants. I did not know what the event or feeling was surrounding this occurrence, but I was confident that a twelve-year-old would persist with his decision, and I doubted that his mother could change his mind. Why fight about something that is within another's control? The parent would not win the fight. I suggested she pick a topic where the pattern was not so strong and work on it, leaving the boy in long pants until the heat dictated a need for change.

For a parent, decisions within the responsibility of children often do not make sense, because adults apply adult standards to them. This can create trauma for children and insoluble problems. As children growing up, we build patterns, partly by watching the reactions of others and partly by our own testing. When an event occurs for which we can't make a decision, or a feeling occurs for which we can't gather data, we want to find an adult who can help us understand it. In either case, if we are unable to resolve the event/feeling, it leaves a hole—an unfinished piece to our pattern—and the hole becomes an attraction. During a discussion about dynamic attractors, a friend remarked, "I have an insight. I've always been attracted to men who were kind of crazy. I don't mean mentally crazy. I mean funny, nutty, strong in a lot of different ways. I just figured out why. My dad was that way and I never really resolved anything with my dad. So I connect with healthy men who do not accept society's rules. My dad didn't accept rules, and I automatically feel attracted to people who want to buck rules." This attraction is an attempt to close the hole in the pattern.

Not only are we attracted by certain unfinished events, we are frightened by them. We want to resolve the event and associated feelings, but if we did, what would happen? We don't know. We feel no sense of control over the event, and yet are drawn to it like a moth to a flame. While we may not feel able to respond to the event, we want to be around people who can respond, so we can try to learn how it's done.

In another relationship with a father, a young man felt that his dad was very difficult to get to know, very hard to please, and very demanding. The young man felt that he was never going to make his father proud. The son suffered through a graduate program and obtained a Ph.D. His father was an M.D., and the young man told himself, "I'm not a real doctor." He felt that way until his father said to him, "I'm proud of you. I think you have done well with your life. I like what you are doing. Would you talk to me about what you do?" This opening allowed new events to occur between the father and son. The father started asking the son for advice. The son was flattered and excited to give his father advice. Prior to the opening offered by his father, the son felt that he would never achieve any success or support from his father. The relationship was not there. When his father gave him permission to close the attractor that was unfulfilled, their relationship began.

Closing Dynamic Attractors

What will it take to change a pattern that is supporting a dynamic attractor? To close the hole caused by a dynamic attractor, the same process of pattern formation is revisited. Our rules also apply. The first rule, *people gravitate to their greatest acceptance,* means that if I do not see or make an opportunity for acceptance between myself and my feelings, the patterns will not change.

In an interview, a person told me about her all-powerful father who ruled the house with an iron hand. Her memory was that he was a huge man, large and intimidating. She remembered that there was no arguing with him, and if she did argue (which she did often) he withdrew his interaction from the whole family for several days. At forty, she chose to change this pattern with her father. She saw her reluctance to confront problems affecting her work. Often, she did not tell others how she felt. She was working to be more assertive. She wanted to visit her father to see how he would accept the "new" assertive woman. She was surprised to find her father was not a huge sulking hulk, but a man of average height. He was very open to talking to her about her childhood, and when she summoned the courage to ask him why he withdrew when there was a conflict in the house, he sheepishly responded, "I always let your mother handle that type of thing." The data of her pattern was based on a small child's knowledge. She judged actions, not causes. Her holes could only be filled with information that was withheld from her.

The second rule is that *nothing happens in isolation*. The woman may have lived her life successfully without ever going home, but she might never have closed the pattern. She would not have had the opportunity to change the outcome had she not revisited the events that caused her feelings. Even though she was coping well on her own, she wanted to change the isolation she felt from her father.

The third rule is that *nothing is random*. In her childhood, this woman had felt terribly responsible whenever her father withdrew. She was sure that she caused it. When she asked her father, his answer to the event was clear and logical. His action had nothing to do with his daughter's *interpretation* of his actions. People do not like ambiguity, and so will invent reasons that things happen. Not only do they invent reasons, they act as if their invention were the truth. Once it is the truth for them, they will want others to participate and will no longer dwell on the event or the feelings. This process explains why different children in the same family do not remember events in the same way. Their problem-solving was different for the same event. Once they have made the decision within their ability to respond, the event no longer needs to be reckoned with.

Patterns and the Subconscious

When a person learns how to problem-solve events and feelings in his life, actions become a pattern. Once the pattern is accepted as the

Pattern Operation and Dynamic Attractors

best way, the way that makes the most sense, the decision-making process goes on autopilot.

This is an unconscious process. Several simple examples of pattern autopilot include a Vietnam veteran's diving for cover when a car backfires, a military cadet's jerking to attention when someone yells attention, or a group of men who duck for cover when someone yells, "Fore!" even if they are not on the golf course. In one environment, all of these actions are functional. Outside the environment, they are autopilot reflexes that appear silly.

Once you go on autopilot, you do not examine your decision anymore. As a child, you often make decisions based on limited capacity (limited by age or maturity) or limited information. In other words, you don't know all your options. But because your decision works, at least marginally, you continue to use it. As you get older, more options open to you, but you still act as if you don't have options.

Suppose you are in a marriage where you fight with your spouse all the time. You still feel like you love your partner, but you fight and argue. Why are you getting that outcome? You are participating in actions that cause that outcome. If you recognize how patterns work, you know that you are responsible for your side of the action. Knowing that you have decided to behave a certain way and taking control of your decision forces you to examine your feelings associated with your actions. This thought process begins to take your actions and decision off autopilot.

If I produce my pattern as a child, my parents accept or reject it. Through their acceptance or rejection, I learn what the boundaries of my actions can be. If I throw tantrums as a child, and my parents reject that action, my tantrums don't work. I try to solve the problem other ways until I find something that does work. Perhaps after I scream and yell, I walk up to my parents and say, "I'm really upset. I have a problem and I would like to talk to you about it. Can we do that?" My parents say, "Sure, that's what we need to do." These actions can develop into a pattern.

When you have an event, you have a feeling, and your decision could be to sit down and work it out logically, or it could be the opposite. If your parents spanked you for having a temper tantrum, you know temper explosions are painful. But if you slipped around your parents, lied, and got what you wanted, those actions could develop into a pattern. If your parents don't reject your actions, you act with their support.

The rejection of a pattern causes conflict. The conflict raises the pattern, or part of it, into our conscious mind until we can problem-solve it again. For this reason, when patterns come into conflict we have the best opportunity to reexamine them. The conflict may be internal because we want to change something personally. Or it may be a conflict with another person or a system.

Operating a pattern in the subconscious only means that we have forgotten the origin of the decision. A friend related that he could not sleep well. He would toss and turn until everyone in the house was safely in bed. Staying awake caused him to be late for work, and when he did arrive, he was in a bad mood. When he began to examine this pattern, he discovered that he had not wanted to go to sleep as a child because his mother and father would fight. He was afraid of the outcome of the fight, that someone would be hurt or leave the family. As a child, he would force himself to stay awake until he was sure that the fight had ended. Now he was carrying on this practice in his own house, away from his parents. He could problem-solve feeling bad the next day because it was in his control. His parents' fighting was not. He only came off of autopilot when he decided that he wanted to sleep better at night.

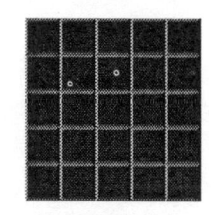

CHAPTER • 11

Pattern Operation:
Power and Change

If you have a pattern, and your pattern doesn't work, it causes a level of tension. The tension could be like a mosquito, just a minor irritation to you. One mosquito is not going to harm you. You don't have to problem-solve it, because it is not causing you enough grief. Suppose fifty mosquitoes are in the room with you. They dive bomb you left and right, biting you through your clothes. They are so bothersome that you can't even sleep. They demand some problem-solving from you. You may pull yourself under the covers, or get up and find bug spray. Your action depends on how much pressure you feel about this irritation.

In many situations, we control our irritation and maintain our position. We may defend this position using a range of patterns. Smoking is a good example. A friend of mine told me one time that when people say they want to quit smoking what they really mean is "I wish I wanted to quit smoking." Let's say doctors tell a smoker that if she doesn't quit smoking it will cause her harm. The irritation of the doctor's advice is not great enough to force her to problem-solve smoking, so she does not quit. If the advice worries her enough, she decides to explore how to solve the problem and quits, therefore changing her pattern.

One good friend did quit smoking. When he quit smoking, he also quit drinking. For him, smoking and drinking were closely connected. He quit hanging out with some of his acquaintances. Because we know that a single behavior is not a pattern, smoking alone is not a pattern. All actions involved are part of the pattern, from before you start to smoke to the end of the cigarette. To the act of smoking, add drinking beer or coffee, add some people to hang out with, conversations with others, reading a good book, watching TV. Each action affects the whole pattern. When one ingredient is changed, the entire pattern is affected. Smoking may be only the most obvious action in a systematic way of doing things. The friend who quit smoking addressed the need to change an entire pattern in order to be successful.

Power and Decisions

At some point, the Golden Rule was cynically rewritten as "the man who has the gold makes the rules." If we rethink it slightly, we recognize that the person who makes the decisions makes the rules. It does not matter whether she is a policemen, a politician, or a parent. The person who makes decisions dictates our range of actions.

In the formation of patterns, a decision is the critical point where a person gains or loses power. To make decisions for myself expands my freedom. Once I develop a pattern, I don't have to think. I am free from the event. I don't go around worrying about it anymore, because I have a pattern that problem-solves it adequately for me. I am not fettered by unwanted feelings; they are under my control. My problem-solving relieves me from worry and gives me successful actions to take when faced with life situations. Problem-solving removes limitations and offers freedom.

Freedom and Responsibility

Freedom demands responsibility. If one has the ability to respond, make a good decision, and carry it out successfully, he is entitled to the freedom accorded the decision. Freedom is a discipline: I have problem-solved my environment. I know the outcome of my actions, and if I remain disciplined in the way I respond, I can consistently have the freedom to make my own decisions. By taking responsibility in a disciplined way, I gain freedom. For a child, doing her homework at the right time gives her extra time to play. For a college student, doing the research on a paper in advance allows her to complete the paper on time. For the businessperson, reviewing the numbers in a timely fashion gives her the time to make sound business decisions.

On the other side, if I make a decision and then am not responsible for it, I'm taking no responsibility to control myself. For example, if I feel that I'm entitled to drive my car as fast as I would like, regardless of the law, of other people, of other cars, then I am taking no responsibility to control myself in the operation of an automobile. Eventually, the result is costly. It may not be costly for me. If the *me* part of the interaction is my only concern, I am taking license. I could kill somebody and not feel bad about it, because I do not see that death as my responsibility. Drunk drivers who kill innocent people and drive drunk again, think this way: "It is not my responsibility. He should have stayed off the sidewalk." The drunk's decision to drive his car on the sidewalk should be accompanied by the responsibility for doing so. If not, the rules about sidewalk driving are useless. The same thinking is true of all rules. If a rule is not applied specifically and consistently, and supported by the community, it is valueless.

Take our prisons, for example. Recently, I heard a man sentenced to three years in prison remark to the judge, "I can do that standing on my head." The deterrent force of prison has been lost because the rules that once applied to prisoners no longer hold. The prisoners run the prison. They have informal group rules that supersede

Life Prescription

prison rules. Once prisoners control the prisons they are able to manipulate the system to their own advantage.

Let's go back to patterns. I am a child. I learn that my parent is not restricted by normal boundaries. For example, my parent does not go to work. The fact that he has the freedom not to work teaches me that I don't need to work. My needs can be taken care of just as my parent's needs are—the check comes in the mail, like magic. This pattern creates license. I have freedom without responsibility.

If I'm a child, I learn from the orientation in my environment. I form a pattern that works. During my early experiences, I am left alone, given too much freedom, and I discover events before I'm able to make sense of (problem-solve) them. I discover sex. I discover alcohol. I discover drugs. What happens if I am able to formulate an action pattern around those discoveries without parental involvement? I learn that I can participate in these activities without consequences. I feel I have the ability to do what I want regardless of what adult authorities tell me. I operate using patterns that adults cannot contradict, and I accept my own ability to do so. In this pattern, I do not see long-range outcomes. I believe the light at the end of the tunnel is an ice cream truck, not a freight train.

In another instance, I see Mom and Dad screaming at each other. Then, Dad leaves. I figure if I scream, somebody will leave. I only scream at those I want to leave. My decision gives me power to eliminate adults who irritate me. By age nine, children who have this permissive pattern believe no adult has the right to tell them what to do. They say, "I'm fourteen years old, and you can't tell me what to do." Nobody has ever successfully rejected that notion. At fourteen, a girl can have a baby if she wants to. Very often, this child's parent has an unresolved dynamic attractor about sex and early relationships, and so the parent does a poor job of rejecting the daughter's actions because the parent has no clear boundary for them. The parent says, "I dropped out of school and got pregnant at fourteen." Unclear resolution for the parent becomes cloudy resolution for the daughter. No one rejects the child's orientation about sex. So, the child explores it too early to problem-solve it properly and must live with the consequences the rest of her life.

When young people rely on an accepting group of peers rather than their parents to orient themselves, they take license with many actions. For example, when children participate in a drive-by shooting, they do not feel any responsibility for the person they shoot or for innocent victims in the line of fire. They don't want to own it. They won't accept it as their decision to kill. If you say to a child, "Why did you do a drive-by shooting?", he is *not* going to tell you, "Because I sat there and planned to kill this person." He will say, "Because I was in the car, they handed me the gun, and we were driving by and I shot him. They said to shoot him and I shot him." Who's "they"? Freedom would be the ability to say, "I don't want to shoot him." Or freedom would be, "I wanted to shoot him, I shot him, and I accept the consequences."

License is freedom without ownership. It is rejecting your responsibility even though you acted on it. Freedom is making a decision and accepting responsibility for it. License is claiming power without choice. Freedom is making choices with responsibility.

Someone taking license is never really free. The pattern that forms around freedom with responsibility is strong, healthy, powerful, and more independent. The pattern that forms around license is dependent, unhealthy, weak, and dangerous to others.

An evolution can occur between license and freedom. As with all pattern changes, the evolution is based on decision. If I have a problem that causes me to feel dependent, I want to overcome it. Sometimes if I change environments and friends, I can problem-solve my dependency in a different way. Let's look at our example of drive-by shootings in this light.

In adolescent circles, boyfriends and girlfriends change. Suppose a conflict occurs, and someone takes another's girlfriend. The person who lost his girlfriend feels rejected. He belongs to a gang. In gang environments (different from home environments), one acceptable solution to rejection is a drive-by shooting. For gangs, drive-by shootings *make sense*. There are a wasteful solution, but they make sense to the people in that sytem. They problem-solve to their satisfaction and there is a reduction of tension. They take responsibility for eliminating a rival suitor or gang member.

In an earlier day, certain groups of adolescents fought a lot. On the north side of Atlanta, there were two major high school groups— Northside High School and Sandy Springs High School. Any time they crossed paths, there was a fight. If you did not want to fight and you went to Northside, you stayed down in Buckhead at Zesto's. If you did not want to fight and you went to Sandy Springs, you stayed around the Sandy Springs bowling alley. If you wanted to fight, you went to the Dunk 'n Dine between Buckhead and Sandy Springs.

When teenagers fought in the sixties, "rules" existed. Everyone understood that you could use a knife, but normally that was outside the boundaries. As the boundaries were tested by fist fighting, then by cutting, and then by shooting, problem-solving options became broader. In addition, in larger metropolitan areas, solutions became more violent, more quickly. In the sixties, guns were not as readily available as today, and if you broke the law, prison was the outcome. Killing was rejected more aggressively by a wider range of people in the sixties than it is now.

The basic problems of territoriality, racial integration, and aggression were never addressed as problems. In football rivalries, adults got into fist fights. On a limited scale, it made sense, but at face value, fighting because you went to different schools was ridiculous. This modeled behavior became the stated reason for fighting among teens, but it was never the true reason. The real reason was a pattern change from teenagers' staying busy working to having leisure time and excessive income.

Unfortunately, if a person is alone in a neighborhood where gangs exist, he is at risk. If there are four gangs in a district, the person is at risk from all four. If he belongs to one gang, he is only at risk from three. To survive, a person had better belong to a gang. Over time, belonging to a gang becomes an autopilot process. The decision is made by the environment and the desire to survive.

The only way to change a pattern is to overcome our own resistance to change, first by understanding what the resistances are, and then by saying, "I don't want this in my life anymore." This becomes a decision that has to be acted on, and we must work through the anxiety associated with that shift by taking action.

Acceptance, Rejection, and Boundaries

In a child's early stages, power falls to the parents. The parents' power is based on their ability (because they are older and have experience) to orient and accept or reject tests offered by the child. The key learning process is the acceptance or rejection of these tests. A two-year-old cries at a school play where older siblings are participating. She is tired. She wants to get down and run to stay awake. But her parents cannot accept this action and remove the child from the play, saying they can return when the two-year-old can control herself (the word most parents use is *behave*).

For children, parental acceptance or rejection is important. One major problem we face in today's society is that parents have abdicated this rejection of inappropriate actions. Parents do not want to damage their children's "self-esteem" by making decisions for them. Often, children are given the latitude to make decisions long before they have the response-ability to do so. Children may be left to decide when they will begin dating. They decide where they will go to school. They decide who their friends will be. Once the orientation is in place and accepted by the child, a parent will have to use excessive pressure to force a change in pattern. A young girl of thirteen is allowed to date. She begins by dating boys her own age, but quickly older boys enter the scene. She has no sexual experience, but may be willing to learn from a boy who offers her acceptance. When that boy appears, she wants to be with him continually. The parents reject that notion, but she has already developed an orientation with dating. Her parents will have a terrible fight on their hands,

Life Prescription

because permissive patterning is hard to reverse. Children know their parents' pattern and manipulate them with it. The child accepts that she is supposed to have the right to make the decisions, and therefore, power over her life. A child with excessive freedom believes the freedom is owed to her. Rarely does she realize she has the power to decide differently and act differently.

CHAPTER • 12

Patterns Uncovered and the Battle Within

How do you identify your own patterns? How do you understand both the "what" and the "how" of your patterns? Understanding what patterns are is one thing, knowing how to uncover them so that you can change them is a different matter.

We know that patterns are developed in a progression. We also know that once you have made a decision and your response works, you tend to eliminate that event or feeling as an irritant in your life. When you reach a situation where you find yourself feeling irritated, you can always backtrack through the process until you find the cause of your irritation. When you find the right event, it will explain a broad range of actions.

Using hypnosis, I helped a woman lose weight. Over the first few weeks, the process worked well. She lost several pounds and was feeling much better. During the third week, she began having difficulty entering hypnosis. She reported that she felt a "block" to relaxing. She also returned to her old eating habits. Nothing in her life had changed to cause this problem. Suspecting she was dealing with an

Life Prescription

autopilot pattern, I suggested that she might find something in her past that caused the "block."

She returned the next week very excited. She reported an insight into her old pattern, and regained control of her eating habits. She related, "I was just going to have some sweets that are on my 'no list' of foods to eat, when an old friend popped into my head. I had had a fight with this friend seven years earlier. I don't even remember what the fight was about, but I never spoke to her again. Before our fight, we were best friends and talked every day. I really missed her. I remembered her telephone number, went to the phone, and called her. I saw her the next day and we started talking again. I love having my friend back. I don't know why I had forgotten about her."

This woman's eating habits were connected to the loss of her friend. The decision not to talk to her friend accompanied her desire to eat. The event that caused the problems between them was long forgotten, but the actions used to cover her feelings were active.

To uncover a pattern one does not require hypnosis: any time you have a feeling or event that causes distress, take time to write down everything that is happening when you get the feeling. Where are you? What are you doing? What are people around you doing? By carefully keeping a record, you can collect six or seven events/actions surrounding your feeling. When you look carefully at everything you've written, a pattern will emerge. Don't get discouraged if you don't see your pattern right away. Ask a friend to look at your list, because often someone who is not as close to a pattern can see it more clearly. When you see the first connections, don't stop. Travel entirely through the pattern development process. Examine it for the problem that the pattern solves.

Patterns give us control and predictability over problems that occur in our lives. As you look at your list, what are you trying to control about the situation? Don't be fooled into thinking that you will only try to control negative occurrences in your life. Whatever the pattern was designed to do, it will do. You were smart when you created it. So, when you interact with your boss, what do you expect? Do you expect him to recognize your hard work just as your teachers/parents did? Do you expect him to find fault? If you expect fault-finding, you'll leave several details undone—just the details he will look for so that you can be less than perfect on the assignment.

One good example of using pattern knowledge to your advantage comes from a friend of mine who opened a restaurant. The renovation process was going slower than he expected. He knew the health inspector was coming on a certain date and the building would not be up to code. He intentionally took out a section of the ceiling over the grill, knowing that this obvious problem would be cited by the inspector. He even went so far as to take him into the grill area first. As expected, the inspector saw the hole above the grill and cited my friend. Over a cup of coffee, they talked amiably. The inspector never looked further at the condition of the restaurant. My friend felt, correctly, that a building inspector's job is to cite something wrong. So he created a glaring error for the inspector to find. Once he had done so, the inspector relaxed and did not cite twenty other flaws under construction. My friend agreed to have the hole over the grill fixed by the inspector's return visit. Within the two-week opportunity, he corrected all the other problems. In the process, he made a friend out of the inspector. By correctly assessing a pattern outcome/expectation, he gained the ability to predict and control that outcome.

As you begin to work on your pattern, think of the event as a freeze frame on a video. You freeze one frame of a videotape, watching for what happens next. If you pay attention, events will lead to feelings, feelings will lead to decisions, decisions lead to responses within your ability, and finally to elimination of the problem. To study your pattern, you can begin anywhere in the process. You may start with a feeling and seek events. You may start with actions (responses) and examine your decisions. Any point in a pattern formation process is a good starting point.

In an earlier example, a mother refused to let her daughter go anywhere alone. Any time the daughter was out of her sight, Mom had a terrible feeling of dread. For a long time, she could never associate that feeling with any event. As a parent, she controlled this feeling by creating multiple protections for her daughter. She gave the daughter a car phone and a beeper, having her call home every hour. The daughter had to check in before and after she went to a movie. I asked her, "What age was your daughter when you first got that feeling?" She answered that the daughter was four years old. I asked her if she could think of any significant event that occurred in the daughter's life at the age of four. She did. The daughter laughed and said, "You've known this for years." Her mother refused to talk about the event so nobody in the family could ever change her mind or actions. When the daughter was four years old playing in the yard, she ran into the street to get a ball. She was struck by a truck and pinned underneath it, and her mother ran out the door just in time to witness the terrible accident. From that point forward, the mother never allowed her daughter out of her sight.

The event caused an extreme fear-reaction for the mother. She made a decision to never allow her daughter out of her sight. Because of that dynamic attractor, as the girl grew older and wanted more freedom, her mother closed down and demanded greater control. The more freedom the daughter wanted, needed, and should have received, the more the mother closed down.

Once we uncovered the event, we examined it realistically for the daughter's ability to take care of herself. Mother had to rethink the problem based on changes in her daughter's ability to assess and keep herself safe from dangers. In this case, our starting point was a parent's restrictive action on a child. Following the responses back through the decision, we found the event. Working through old feelings gives us an opportunity to assess whether the present situation warrants the old response or realistically calls for us to make a new decision.

As you begin to look at change, remember that changes are charged with emotion. Your pattern will resist change—*you* will resist change. You have to act through your feelings to achieve success.

Guidelines for Changing Your Pattern

1. Become Aware

Part of self-improvement is simply the desire to know. It leads to a recognition that we all work in patterned ways and need to examine our patterns from time to time. Periodic examination and maintenance is preferable to waiting until some part of the pattern stops working for us.

When trauma occurs, we are forced to face limits in our patterns and renew problem-solving. Trauma can be a death, a sudden change in fortune, or a reversal in relationships. We become aware that some part of our pattern is not working. The pattern is not getting us what we want.

Awareness can come from other people, from actions that no longer work, or from feelings we cannot eliminate. No matter what form awareness takes, use it as a sign to begin problem-solving. Take the situation as a problem to be solved, rather than an immovable obstacle. In a tiger hunt, cloth is stretched out to enclose the shooting area for the hunters. The tiger is driven into the cloth enclosure. Because the tiger does not challenge the cloth (which he could easily shred), he is trapped and shot. Don't make the same mistake and assume that barriers cannot be challenged.

Awareness is not an action. Awareness is a feeling. What you are saying is, How does an itch get to the point where you would scratch it? First, you know it itches. What do you do? The first step is to put your finger on the spot. Next, move the finger left and right. But, questions arise. Do you ever put your finger exactly on the itch or do you scratch a general area? In the same regard, an irritant in a pattern should cause you to say to yourself, "There exists a problem that I need to solve."

2. Gather Data

Gather data about the series of events that brought this feeling or this awareness to you. If, for instance, you wake up in the morning and

Life Prescription

you don't want to get out of bed: what is it you are supposed to do? Whom are you supposed to meet? How are you supposed to be carrying yourself? What are you supposed to accomplish? What is expected of you? Gather data around the feeling. You don't want to get up, but why? What is it you don't like? Or, what is it you think doesn't like you? What are all the things that are going on around you?

Gathering data is an orientation. Just as we described a child watching and learning patterns, an aware person orients himself to his problem. Orientation works to gather facts and organize them into a real picture of the problem. As the picture emerges, you are able to become directed, to attack the problem with facts.

3. Decide What to Do

In the story of the prodigal son, the young man left his father's house with all his money and squandered it. After the money was gone, he was hired by one of his buddies to feed the swine and began thinking about eating pig food. Finally, the story began to change as he had a realization: "And he came to himself." So, what a person does is decide, "I own this orientation. I own these facts. I own this problem in my life." After I recognize everything about the problem, I decide to own it.

Do you know what that implies? It implies that you are absent from yourself, performing on autopilot, without thinking about whether the pattern is working to get you what you want. Once you recognize this and make a decision that you will not use your old pattern, you must create a new pattern.

This point is when most people quit. Their old pattern may not be working just right, but maybe it's only tired. What is the new pattern? We don't know yet. Will it work? Who knows? I can give a good example from my own experience. At this point in my life I have probably thirty unfinished books around my office. I have written parts of books about handling kids in a classroom, teaching, parenting, psychotherapy, business operation, psychology/physics, personality theory, and team operation. To finish this book, I needed a new pattern.

My first step was to say to my office team, "I will own the fact that I can't finish a book. I will own the fact that this company needs a book written. I want you (team) to help me problem-solve writing a new book, because my tension gets too high to problem-solve by myself." The team helped me talk through the event and my feelings. We worked on a new decision and a new way to implement it. I began working on the book.

The first few attempts did not work because of my old pattern. I took the problem back to the team and we came up with an innovative solution that has produced a change in my pattern, made writing a pleasurable event for me, and pushed the book forward.

4. Act on Your Decision

To change my actions, I plan what I think will produce my desired outcome. Then I act on it. I do it. As I move forward, I adjust my actions until I can consistently achieve my goal.

While you are acting and adjusting your actions to achieve the goal, what happens to your feelings? At first, feelings drive anxiety up. As tension increases, the new actions drive problem-solving down (remember the chart in Chapter 9). People want to go back to their old patterned response—the pattern that is comfortable for them. They must continually renew their commitment to newly learned actions.

During this action period, I am stretching my response-ability. I am learning new limits, adjusting to new tension levels. For example, perhaps I do not like fancy dress dinners, but my new job requires me to attend them. I must go to the dinners. I could avoid the event and control my feelings. If I do, I can't achieve the goal of doing my job. If I go and isolate myself, no improvement occurs in my ability to socialize at these gatherings. I have to go, stick my hand out, smile, and make friendly with the natives.

The only way to change a pattern is *to act* on your decision to change. Action replaces feelings when you are actively problem-solving. Tension is reduced by acting, moving, adjusting, and learning. Pushing yourself to step out, walk across the room, put a hand out, smile, and watch the reaction of other people produces change. Immediately, you discover they react well. You are now succeeding.

Here is another example: If you don't have very much confidence in your speaking ability, you can prepare and plan great speeches, but if you don't get up in front of three hundred people and give that speech, you will never know if you can. Even though your legs are shaking, your voice is quaking, your hand is shaking on the microphone, you can't give up. You have to get up, force yourself to speak expressively, and force yourself to play a little with the audience. Only then will you know whether you can give that speech. If you force yourself again and again and again, eventually you will know what success is when you give a speech.

5. Let Go

Did you ever have to climb a tree to rescue a cat? You reach the cat and take hold of it, but it won't let go. Its claws are dug in to the tree, and you have to physically detach it. People can be like that about their patterns if they have not chosen to change them. But once you have made your choice, your actions make the transition easier. It actually feels good to see consciously chosen patterns replace those created when you did not have adequate information.

The last and most rewarding part of change is letting go of unneeded patterns and replacing them with active, functional ones. The negative feelings created by your old patterns vanish. In a high-ropes course, people climb forty-foot poles and perform actions at the top, such as standing up on top without holding on. When we were teenagers, this type of activity was common—we were daredevils. When we are forty years old, few chances come our way to stand on top of a forty-foot pole and say, "Look, Ma, no hands." People are frightened of this activity, but act *through the fear.* They remember the event as a success, even though it was initially a negative, fearful situation. Because they succeed, people feel good to have survived it. Pattern elimination is the same: if everybody understood that patterns can be overcome and controlled, the outcome would be great.

Naming a Pattern

When you work to understand your patterns, you will be tempted to give them names. Eric Berne, in his book *Games People Play*, did a masterful job of naming faulty interaction patterns. But it doesn't really matter if you can name a pattern. What matters is whether you see actions, understand what outcomes they produce, and change them. Sometimes when you name a pattern, you can make change harder, because you have given the pattern an identity outside your control that you have to overcome. In reality, what is it that you are overcoming? You. So, why would you want to create a separate new identity? What do I want to wrestle myself for? The process of pattern change is hard enough without complicating it.

One clear way to see this phenomenon is in the "victim mentality pattern" that our culture supports. Anyone who does not want to own his behavior can claim he is a victim. The person who gets lung cancer after smoking for twenty-five years sues the tobacco company. The person who drinks too much and has a wreck, sues the bar that served the drinks. These examples have a clear theme: "I do not have the ability to respond and you must have sneaked into my life and made my decisions for me." These individuals claim to be victims. In reality, most are opportunistic con artists who want to avoid ownership of their decisions.

The Battle Within

No matter what patterns you have learned early in life, you can change them. Suppose I have a strong, overpowering desire to drink. If I call my AA sponsor rather than take a drink, I know I can be with someone who will help me talk through my feelings and perhaps help me change my decision about drinking. If I decide to call rather than drink, I change my response. I break the pattern with the help of a stronger person. A different decision and response make the outcome different. The new outcome moves me closer to a goal of sobriety versus a goal of drunkenness.

Life Prescription

This beginning is hopeful, but must be adjusted. I am confident I want to drink no more. I have had success problem-solving by using my sponsor, but I want to control the pattern myself. All the people around me—my friends, my spouse—have a pattern of drinking. My lifestyle is built around this habit: when we get together we drink. Do I have to give up my whole lifestyle? What I *must* give up is my old decision—the decision that says I can drink. I have to be strong enough to socialize with my friends who drink and to say I want club soda. If I cannot be with them and order club soda, I cannot socialize with them. I must either eliminate the event (social gatherings with alcohol) or the feeling (I crave a drink).

This process takes us back to problem-solving. There are events in every individual's life that create stress: making good grades, being outgoing socially, dating and sex. They are unknowns that all of us have to problem-solve. One way to relieve the stress of problem-solving is alcohol.

A person may learn to drink from parents, friends, or on his own. No matter how it evolves, drinking becomes a pattern. A decision is made to drink. In the same regard, there can be a decision to quit. In psychology, they tell us that for every stimulus there is an immediate response. What is true is that when an event occurs and it creates a feeling, it puts us in a problem-solving mode. As in the earlier example, I could go with my friends and order a club soda or a Coke. I could join them and be a designated driver. I could be with some of them because they do not drink as heavily as others, and be accepted for not drinking. There are multiple ways to decide and respond. Having the ability to respond differently eliminates the need to use alcohol to reduce tension.

In a different scenario, you could sit down and say, "I have been drinking for a number of years and I don't see anything particularly productive about it, so I'll quit." If your friends are your friends, they accept your decision. Control of your life is yours, not theirs. At each step, we may go back to feeling as helpless and useless as a child until we make our decision. Decision always brings control.

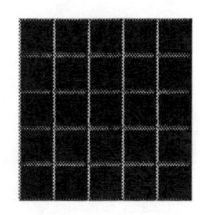

CHAPTER • 13

Building Healthy or Unhealthy Patterns

As we grow up, we can build healthy or unhealthy patterns. The pattern doesn't care. A pattern wants an outcome that problem-solves and releases tension. Your pattern is there to make you feel better. Until later, when you interact with other people and the pattern doesn't work, right or wrong is unimportant. The worst example I can think of occurred when a young couple was arrested on suspicion of child abuse. Their three-year-old daughter walked up to a friendly police officer and grabbed him by the penis. She asked in a coy voice, "Can I be your friend?" Her parents had trained her to perform sexual acts. She thought that this was the approach that a male adult would accept. But it didn't work as it did with her parents. The officer was terrified and disgusted. Because no one in her environment had ever acted that way before, the child was surprised.

Life Prescription

Building Healthy Patterns in Children

Healthy patterns are created by healthy interactions. Any child has a range of possible interactions within the environment. As parents provide for a child's basic needs—at a minimum, food, shelter, and clothing—other information is being passed between parent and child. This provides a basic pattern orientation that helps the child learn about the world and how it operates.

Parent/Child Pattern Orientation

	Child Learns	Child Does Not Learn
Parent Knows	Learns from the parent	Withheld from the child
Parent Does not know	Learns from another source	Unknown

This diagram illustrates parent-child interactions. In the upper-left box, the child is trying to learn and the parent knows what to teach. This range of information can be positive or negative. As we saw in the example above, parents who are sick can teach a sick orientation to a child. Parents who are decent people teach their children that they can trust their basic needs to be cared for, and that they will receive emotional care equal to the physical care. The range

Building Healthy or Unhealthy Patterns

of the orientation is what the parents know about the environment and what they think is necessary for a child to know.

In the upper-right box, the child is willing to learn, but the information is not presented because it is not age appropriate or the parents have a particular feeling about the subject matter. This may include religious information. I have Jewish friends who do not teach their children about Santa Claus because it is not part of their belief system. This information may become available later, but not through the parents' input.

In the lower left box, the child learns information that the parents do not know he will receive. Such information may come from teachers who are more educated than the parents. It may come from TV or from computers, technology that was not part of the parents' orientation when they were growing up. These facts are beyond the parents' knowledge.

In the fourth, lower right quadrant is information beyond the awareness of both parent and child. It may be outside their environment and/or beyond their capabilities. These areas might include world politics or the monetary policy of the United States. Without a special interest or education, neither parent nor child would know about or understand these topics.

In the second part of building a healthy pattern, a child tests what he is learning. The child formulates the test to gain success and control within the environment. The outcome of this part of the interaction is depicted in the following chart (see page 88).

The boxes in this chart show what happens when a child acts on the orientation he has received. In the upper-left box, the child produces an action that meets his parents' approval. In behavior modification parlance, this acceptance would be a positive reinforcement, and it would probably lead the child to continue to test the action, refining its success until it became a pattern. Suppose a child ran in and gave her parent a hug and kiss. The parent's response would be joyful and accepting. Or a parent might reward his child, who had behaved politely to a family friend, by buying him a surprise gift. Parents reward actions they feel are good with praise and acceptance.

Life Prescription

Parent/Child Pattern Testing

Child's Action

		Works in the world	Does not work in the world
Parent's Reaction	Accepts	Child gains successful pattern	Child gains false success; only one environment
	Rejects	Child confused; must test further	Child gains clear boundary

In the upper right box, a child tries an action that does not work, but the parent does not reject it. Perhaps she tries to make breakfast for her parent. The result is a wrecked kitchen, burnt toast, and spilled orange juice. But the parent recognizes the attempt as a positive action and does not stop it. Because of the parent's acceptance, the child may not recognize her failure. She may try again in the future and in fact, may grow up to be a successful chef. On the other hand, if the child does recognize her failure, she may wait before trying to cook again.

In the lower left box, the child's test actions succeed, but the parent is not impressed and clearly rejects the child's actions. Under normal circumstances, the child may repeat the action to see if his parent's rejection was real. If the parent is not consistent with a negative reaction, the child may learn to do something that the parent does not want him to do. My son, for example, is fascinated by a creek in our backyard. He is only allowed to visit it with me. Recently, when he was with a babysitter, he went to the creek, not telling her it was off limits without an adult. We only knew what he had done because of his muddy shoes. The babysitter did not tell us about the rule breach because she did not know about that limit. If we had not recognized the clue (muddy shoes), confronted his action (going down to the creek alone), and rejected it as inappropriate, he would have considered it an acceptance and he would have tested the system again (gone back to the creek alone). Instead, we were able to reject what he considered a success.

This box reflects the beginning of the classic game of "divide and conquer." If I do not get the right answer from Mom, I ask Dad.

The final, lower-right box depicts an ill-formed test followed by resounding rejection. When a child tries to cross the street before his parents feel he is able, their response is firm and clear. Normally, the child will not attempt such an action again. A friend's two-year-old daughter, for example, constantly poked her fingers near the slot on the family's VCR. Her parents worried for her fingers. They sat quietly while she explored near the slot, and when she got too close, both voiced a resounding, "NO!" The child was frightened. She cried and withdrew from the VCR, not to touch it again for several years. Her failure to touch the slot and the strong rejection worked to keep her fingers well out of harm's way.

At one time or another in the pattern-building process, we will visit every box in our two charts. As children, we will make the most progress in the boxes that offer the greatest orientation, which is when our tests are accepted. Once we become parents, we will accept the tests with which we are most familiar. So, we come full circle, and actions are transferred from one generation to the next.

Specific, Consistent, Supportive

Healthy actions and interactions have three components: they are specific, consistent, and supportive. One can see the evolution of these components in the charts above. Specifics occur between people when the orientation and testing matches, which is then accepted by the parent. The details follow as an adjustment to the tested actions. When a child walks into a classroom with a chip on his shoulder, teachers can pick him out immediately. A good teacher knows that within the first few hours this child will test her. The test is to see if the pattern of intimidation and aggression that he uses outside the classroom and with other teachers will work in this room. The tests vary. The child will not get out a book when told. He may get up and wander to the back of the room without permission. The child may talk out, perhaps making a smart remark to his peers during the lesson. A good teacher sees this test coming and handles it long before it starts.

To make this test into a healthy interaction, the good teacher stops the child at the door. The teacher sets ground rules with the child and follows the agreed-upon rules specifically. Specifying the orientation about the class stops the testing behavior, gives the child an opportunity to be accepted, and allows success to become the basis of the classroom interaction.

Healthy Patterns in Adults

In the workplace, the same actions apply. In this arena, the test will not be as overt. Workers will watch to see if any difference exists in the way people take breaks or come to work, or the way managers watch workers. Any difference may be exploited by a few employees.

Clear and specific operating instructions create clear boundaries, whether between workers and managers or parents and children. Clear boundaries make actions more successful. People get to win when they know what to do and specifically how to do it.

When actions are consistent, people know how to do their job successfully. Consistency is not boring but exciting because everyone knows how to do his job. On a military drill team, members of the team march slowly with their rifles held across their chests. At the leader's command, the first person throws a rifle complete with bayonet over his shoulder (without looking) to the tenth man in the line. The tenth man catches the rifle, and everyone continues marching slowly, as if nothing had happened. This difficult maneuver looks so smooth and easy that it seems anyone can do it.

Because everyone in a system knows what to do and how to do it,

Building Healthy or Unhealthy Patterns

each supports the other to reach the goal. Just as a parent becomes more supportive of a child doing "right and expected" actions, any group gets behind its members when they are working toward a common goal. This support allows the members to risk new ways of doing things that are consistent with the healthy promotion of the team.

We can look for these three attributes in any pattern. In a business meeting, are the people trying to specify the tasks, are they using consistent techniques to attack problems, are they supporting other's successes? In a classroom, are the students given exact assignments, are they given adequate instructions, are questions answered? In a family, does everyone know the ground rules, can anyone bring up a problem, are they supported as the family searches for an answer? Such healthy interaction is critical to independent growth and strength.

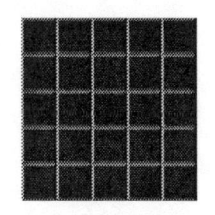

CHAPTER • 14

A Healthy Pattern Process in Life

Everyone lives his own life. This seemingly obvious statement has several interesting aspects. First, it implies that being a participant in your life is not a choice. From birth you are living and growing. In a pattern, each movement is individual. Each person grows and chooses to stop problem-solving when he wants. Once we have solved all the elementary problems of life, it may appear that there is nothing left to do. At this point, some people dull their awareness (go on autopilot) to attend only to those occurrences they already know how to handle. They pay no attention to issues outside their chosen range. This closure offers control and immediate comfort, but creates a gap between what is real and what the person chooses to attend to. This gap may not ever bother some people. They may find friends who tolerate their behavior, participate only in activities and organizations that support their beliefs, and feel that they have vast control over their lives.

One clear example of this is in family businesses. The family business opens when one family member has the vision and insight required to begin a business. If he is successful, he brings fortune and fame to the family. The business may be anything from building cars to extorting money from other small companies. As the founder ages, passing the mantle from generation to generation can become unwieldy. Children growing up in the lap of luxury do not have the same drive to problem-solve business issues that the founder did. Resentments follow. Recriminations consume the relationships until the founder, who believes he started the business for his children, cannot understand their avoidance of business operation. The founder never thinks how the problems he had to solve building the business differ from the problems he eliminated for his offspring by his hard work.

Growth is developmental. As we pass through the *event, feeling, decision, responsibility, and elimination* process of pattern development, we inevitably reach milestones that indicate our progress. Erik Erikson explained that each person begins life by gaining a sense of *basic trust*. Basic trust allows us to believe that our needs will be fulfilled by those around us, that we can rely on others for help, and that we can learn to trust ourselves in accomplishing tasks.

Success and trust open our desire to do a task on our own. We want to succeed by ourselves. "Don't hold the bike anymore." "Let me hit the nail." "I want to write this report by myself." Trusting that we have a skill, we want the *autonomy* to exercise it. This successful action leads to trying other new things on our own. We take *initiative*. We seek challenges that test our solutions about life. We learn to be *industrious* in our actions, sticking to a task until we work it all the way to a success. Our ability to persist and overcome gives us an *identity*. We know ourselves by the tasks we can perform and the successes we can produce. In like manner, we seek to identify with others who have similar thinking and behavior. We gravitate into intimate relationships with others of like mind and we work to educate those who disagree with us. Being successful, we try to give something of our skill back to others. We trust that we are strong and capable without having to be reminded. We organize our actions in the most advantageous manner for ourselves and others. We treat people with an open, unafraid spirit, knowing that we are successful at our lives and wanting others to achieve that success also.

A Healthy Pattern Process in Life

For a child just forming patterns in his life, each stage is a mountain. To climb to its peak requires a guide. In the child's life, the adult is the guide. It does not matter what the range of experience or education the parent has. What is of paramount importance is what kinds of problems the child faces and the way his parents help him to find a solution.

In England during World War II, families often had to run for the safety of the bomb shelters. While they were underground, some families distracted the children from the sounds and carnage above by playing games and singing songs. Other families sat quietly fearful for their homes, belongings, and their lives. When they grew up, the wartime children had very different memories. While one group remembered the panic and fear, others remembered their time together as a family, and they did not remember it as traumatic. Childhood trauma survivors' experiences are similar. It appears that if there is a strong supportive adult in the life of the child, the long-term effects of the trauma are diminished.

Building basic trust requires being consistent between word and deed. If I tell a child something is going to happen, it must happen. Say a newly divorced father promises his son, "I will pick you up Saturday morning and we will go fishing," When Saturday morning comes, the parent fails to arrive.

If the parent has a pattern of disappointing a child, the child may resolve this problem by constantly forgiving him, because he always behaves this way. The child learns not to depend on his father and often ends up being the one who has to reassure him. This action is not an uncommon way to work out basic feelings of distrust, so that one can keep the relationship. The child may solve the problem of not asking anything of that parent, by avoiding him, or by waiting, depending on how patient he is. He will try a number of difference actions, based on his age, to solve the problem.

Often, when distrust is the basis of a relationship, kids blame themselves for their parent's actions (divorce, etc.). Why? Because in the early stages when the child was developing a pattern, he couldn't solve the problem. He couldn't fix it between Mom and Dad. He thought if he could only find the magical solution, if the wizard would come and wave the magic wand, if only the white horse would come, he could then be strong enough to fix a bad pattern that actually belonged to his parent, not to him. As the child grows older and the parent continues to act out that pattern, the child becomes a participant in not being able to solve it.

If a child has learned trust, and his parents divorce, he may also feel responsible. If a trusting child heard his parents say, "This is not your fault. It's our fault. You had nothing to do with it," the child may believe it. But it is a new problem, a new orientation that has to be tested.

Emotionally healthy parents who divorce provide a strong, supportive network so that the child can continue in a trusting relationship with both parents. Neither parent berates or abuses the other. They sit down with their child and say, "We love you." And then they live it. The father comes on time and the mother gives him up willingly. She is happy that he has a relationship with his father. The father is happy that he has a strong relationship with his mother. If other romantic relationships enter the picture, at worst, the divorced parents tolerate them. They may never be best friends with each other, but they are supportive of their child in a healthy way, and in fact, a child can learn healthy patterns from his parent's divorce.

Building trust is the beginning of developing a healthy pattern. Trust is built through living these ideas: "I'm going to show you a good pattern. I'm going to tell you a good pattern, and I'm going to live it. When you start to emulate it, I'm going to support and accept you. When you start to emulate a bad pattern, I'm going to reject it. I'm going to coach you as to how to come back to positive problem-solving."

For example, one child was having difficulty in school. He was behind in his classes, and he received an F on his progress report. His parents thought it was wrong for the teacher to give him an F when he had tests to make up, and they asked for a conference with the teacher.

The child had listened to his parents' conversations as they gathered

A Healthy Pattern Process in Life

information about his situation, talking on the telephone to teachers, principals, and other parents. As his parents met with his teacher, the child played on the playground. When they left the conference, the boy asked his father if he could go to a different school. When asked why, he answered, "Because nobody likes me." When asked what he meant, he just said he wanted to go to another school. Finally he said, "Because the principal doesn't like me." His parents asked him to explain and he said, "Well, she just doesn't like me." "How do you know?" "Because my teacher told her that I wasn't doing good in school and because you went and had a meeting with her." The child thought that the principal was in the meeting (she was not). His solution to this process was to "run away," to change schools.

Let's make a connection between this event and an earlier one in this child's life. This child was adopted when he was fourteen months old. His new dad was drinking a Coke and set it down on the table where the child could reach it. The father saw him lifting the Coke and shouted, "No!" The boy put the Coke down, but a terror-stricken look came over his face. He ran across the room and body slammed himself into a two-foot square between the piano and the wall.

This was the same pattern he used in response to the situation at school. He ran away. When he felt pressure from the school and thought that the people didn't like him, he wanted to run to another school. Allowing him to do that would be accepting an unhealthy pattern.

Prior to talking about the school situation, the child would not tell his parents anything about school. He was so upset and tense that he wouldn't talk. After the teacher conference, the father spent the evening talking with the child about school and discovered his fear. The boy was afraid he would not be liked by the teacher, his parents, or the principal. The father corrected his fears. After the discussion, the boy did all of his homework, went to school the next day, and passed his test.

The child had experienced an event, a terrible feeling, and could not make a decision because he had never seen it modeled any other way. But in this incident, his father coached him to a healthy solution and was specific and supportive through the process. Dad showed him another way.

As we discussed earlier, the child's first and best response at the time was to run, which would have eliminated the source of his anxiety. Running had solved a problem for him in the past or he wouldn't have used it again. The child learned this pattern originally from the people he had lived with. At one point, he witnessed his primary caretaker attempt suicide. At another point, he was left alone to eat whatever he could find. His basic solution to things that were too big for him to control or predict was to run. He would run from the people that he used to live with in order to get away from their yelling and screaming. He transferred that solution to a later point in his life, and it would have continued to be his preferred solution if his new father hadn't helped him find a healthier option.

The purpose of a pattern is to produce an outcome that makes a person feel in control and give him a sense of predictability. In patterns, there is no right or wrong, only what works. This is especially true if parents are using the same pattern as their children. If parents are dealing drugs and using their child as a look-out, the child is never going to question drug dealing. As in the earlier example of the three-year-old who was taught by her parents to perform sexual acts for them, the child thought that everything she was doing was successful because she was accepted for it.

The Final Choice

Each person has control over his life. The degree of this control varies within its context. A POW, for example, does not have much freedom within the confines of a prison camp, but he can make decisions within the area over which he does have control. He can create a code to talk to other prisoners. If he is creative, he can communicate without being caught. He can refuse to cooperate with efforts to make him reveal information about his fellows. He can choose to die. In *Man's Search For Meaning*, Victor Frankel relates that in Nazi concentration camps, people would choose to die. Physically, he says, they were no worse off than their comrades, but when they lost hope and meaning about the suffering they endured, they chose to quit life, and died. People always have control over their decision, even though they may feel overpowered.

The *values and standards* that you expect from your life are up to you, and the patterns that you build around them to reach those expectations are up to you. You learn what you can accept or reject from the patterns of your parents. Suppose there were certain things that your parents would never let you even imagine doing, but a situation arose later where those things became possibilities. Odds are you would not even think about doing them. But someone else who learned a different acceptance or rejection level from his parents, would throw different ideas into the mix.

When you accept or reject something, you do so based on what you have learned. You have created a pattern to support your process of accepting and rejecting. When you say, "I can't give a speech," you reject yourself as a speaker, which then alleviates your anxiety. It all goes back to *event, feeling, decision, responsibility, elimination.*

Child Decision and Adult Decision

When you are a child, you are told to do things in a certain way. You are told to do what is right. But the way you've done things comes from a child's way of doing things as opposed to an adult way. To change your pattern, you have to change from the child's patterns to those of an adult.

Most people believe that they are acting in an adult way. The question is whether the pattern is even perceived as wrong. A person who explodes might feel perfectly justified in blowing up at another person. We assume that the person feels some remorse. But he has learned that explosive reactions work and so far, nothing has contradicted that learning. This thinking could be applied to children who are involved in juvenile court systems across America. They have learned patterns that worked in their environment. They do not feel that their actions are incorrect. Often they feel the system is unjust for catching them and trying to punish them for their crimes.

When I realize I am getting an outcome that I do not want, I must examine the situation. For example, a husband and wife may argue and fight daily, although they love each other. Why are they getting this result from their marriage? Each person is participating in something that causes the outcome to move forward. Each is responsible for at least one side of the action, which means that they are deciding to behave or act in that particular way.

Once we accept that the way we act represents a *decision,* we can take control of that decision and examine our feelings driving the process. This examination is painful. People consider their feelings of discomfort an inward battle. They try to stop acting on the decision that they made years ago when their actions made them successful. The battle is knowing in your heart what is right to do but holding to the way you have always acted. When people realize their pattern, they grow and mature by problem-solving and struggling to change. This struggle creates an adult problem-solving pattern.

A feeling of discomfort comes when you do something that doesn't make sense. If you have that feeling about an occurrence, go back and look at the event as if it were a moving picture. Based on the way you have problem-solved historically, there was an event that originally caused that discomfort. To solve that uneasy feeling, you made a decision in your past and it worked. You acted on your decision—not just made the decision, but performed an action in association with it. You were able to produce a response, such as a tantrum.

As a child, you may have found that after a tantrum, you did not have to eat your spinach. You got what you wanted. As an adult, when you go to work and an individual challenges your proposal, you feel that same unease and the old decision kicks in. The explosion takes place on an adult level, and the other person wanders off muttering under his breath. Even though you did not really mean to treat your colleague in such a way, the sense of relief you experience because the pattern worked is stronger than the remorse you feel for having made someone angry.

Every day, new opportunities arise for us to see ourselves as problem-solvers. Accepting that we are response-able to decide and act differently gives us greater control and independence.

CHAPTER • 15

The Big Picture

In the 1985 movie *Creator*, Dr. Harry Wolper spends much of his time telling everyone they must understand the "Big Picture." Still desperately in love with his deceased wife, Dr. Wolper tries to clone her. Oblivious to rules around him, he is successful, but he stops his work when he discovers love coming into his life in new forms. Life does not wait for his wife to return.

Wolper has a clear belief that if he follows a particular system in a disciplined way, he can recapture life for his dead wife. He is disciplined in following that path until the system intervenes and destroys his soon-to-be-successful "experiment." At one critical point in the film, he declares to the governmental officials who have provided his grant, "As you know, we do research on the biological mechanisms of disease. And this morning, I am pleased to announce that God has agreed to provide us with all the answers we need for just under $800,000."

Is this true? Can we have the secrets for money? No. We can have them for free. All answers are available for the adept student of pat-

Life Prescription

terns—anyone who wants to live his life in the wonder of discovery about himself and patterns around him.

In the "Big Picture," truth is the reality that cuts between a real systematic improvement and a temporary respite from the "old way" of doing things. Truth is found in facts. Facts are simply "what is." If I wanted to know the yield of a restaurant, I need to start with the known facts about the restaurant. For example, what is the square footage? How are the tables laid out? How many people can sit at each table? We need to know the labor costs, food costs, fixed costs, and gross income for the restaurant. These facts give us a real picture of the business, and we can begin to understand how it should operate.

The truth is in the facts of everyday life. These facts inform us of choices. The choices are the force we put into decisions to create success either in a restaurant business or in our lives. Making decisions on facts gives us control of the outcome.

In one situation, a company had a number of business contracts. One was with the State of Oregon, which required that all cases shipped to them have a certain label and number. The machine that labeled and numbered the cases repeatedly malfunctioned. When this happened, an order was issued to send the part out to be repaired. It was a common routine and had occurred many times in the past. Finally, the problem arose again and was brought up in a meeting. The discussion was drifting toward the same conclusion, when one of the floor workers raised his hand. He sheepishly asked, "Do we still have the Oregon contract?" This simple question silenced the whole management group. The Oregon contract had been canceled four years earlier. All the trouble and expense to keep the labeling machine operational had been unnecessary. A simple fact rendered obsolete the decision that had controlled the operation for the last four years.

Having the facts gives us information about how to control actions in our lives. This ability to establish the facts and to separate essential from non-essential facts is the basis of problem-solving. Using facts and problem-solving skills, an adult can extrapolate meaning from the trends and patterns of facts. This skill is given to all of us. It is the skill of finding meaning in actions.

Meaning comes to those who work for it. Making sense is a key ingredient in how we can live and must live if we are to improve our lives. Improvement is an ongoing process—an expanding circle. It expands to encompass larger and larger truths seen in the way they play out on the stage of life.

The mastery of problem-solving occurs when we can, almost intuitively, establish the facts and act appropriately on our decision. In a plant, the individuals who can tell a machine is running badly by sound, vibration, or quick observation has valuable experience that helps the plant to solve problems quickly. When new machines are installed, a period of time passes before these individuals can perform the same magic with the new machines. This is merely the orientation and testing period of the new machine.

Changing to Remain the Same

Scientists experiment with life in a test tube. They create, change, clone, and isolate the information that codes life and makes it become what it is. They splice together different characteristics and produce different genetic combinations—a disease-free tomato here, a faster-growing pine tree there.

This experimentation and its success on the level of genetics is the same interference that other animals have experienced for years. We have controlled breeding of animals to produce "improved stocks." We have developed cows that produce more milk and gain weight more quickly, cats that have no fur, large dogs, fierce dogs, small dogs, and dogs with shinier coats. Man has made them all. We have manipulated the process of natural selection to suit our specific preferences. Then, we protect the new mutations from the aspects of the environment which would harm them. Man ensures that they are fed, so there is no competition for food. Man ensures their breeding, so there is no competition for a mate or territory.

Systematically we exploit our knowledge for our own pleasure. Is

Life Prescription

this a bad thing? I don't know, but it feels wrong when we examine it from the perspective of patterns. Factually, we know that a systematic pattern occurs in the life and death of all living things. Once an organism attains life, it does not easily give up. The grizzly bear's habitat has been reduced to a small area from what was once all of North America. So the bear fights back. Grizzly bear attacks on man are increasing. The act of fighting back is what all organisms do when they are forced to change their pattern.

Animals or systems that can adapt do so. Raccoons, armadillos, and possums all have become common sights in places where they were once rare. More recently, foxes and coyotes have spread into inhabited areas. They are using the garbage and refuse of society to problem-solve their continued existence.

In the same way, systems that have evolved to a point of independent life are slow to adapt. The system can be IBM or the federal government. In the case of IBM, the corporation was so large and so successful that no one on the inside saw the devastating economic competition coming. IBM had its own language that outsiders found difficult to understand. It had its own way of doing business. It was an arrogant way, refusing to see any of the changes that would ultimately force the company to completely reorganize. Only when the problem threatened its very existence did IBM start to problem-solve the situation. Top management was incapable of thinking about it and had to be removed before any substantial change took place. They had taken the lead in assuring stockholders that nothing major was wrong and that, over time, no action was the best course.

As for the government, an excess of money has created a feeling that nothing can go wrong. The leaders of this monster have always calmed themselves with the reassurance that taxes must be paid and the government will survive. It is at the heart of patterns that both of these giants cannot survive. They are like an animal secure in its hole that does not adapt or problem-solve further. This lack of activity produces a lethargy and indifference to cries for change from outside.

The Nixon Cabinet exemplified the problem, not at its height, but at its most vulnerable point. In a pattern, the public and press had decided not to participate in the actions of a corrupt, or as I have heard it stated, "morally challenged" administration. The result was not to stop with the small fish in the process, which had indeed worked in the past. How many chief officials of companies, knowing what goes on, have offered up lower-level officials as sacrificial lambs? In the past, such offerings worked: they problem-solved the chief's issues and allowed him to continue in office. This time and since then, the cost has been higher. Only if the public and private sector wish to participate in the lies they are told, can that cost be avoided.

Here are some simple examples of changing to remain the same.

Downsizing

In business and government, the idea of downsizing has become popular. In business, it is considered essential. Businesses that have experienced downsizing have often ignored the patterns of their culture. They have acted as if the profit of the company is primary, and this has resulted in an interesting change in internal operations.

The focus has been on cutting costs to improve the bottom line. The form is to find jobs to cut and reorganize positions so that teams of people can take over tasks previously reserved for individuals. This requires two major pattern changes in business: First, businesses have to share information and data with the team doing the job. Information is power. With the advent of the computer, this is true now more than ever before. A team of people must know what it is to do and have the facts before it can make good, high-quality decisions. Second, the entire management process must decentralize to accommodate the new operations. Leadership must function in context with what is occurring.

To solve the problem of becoming more globally competitive, business has sacrificed people and control as never before. Unfortunately, this change has a price. Businesses needed guidance to move from the old pattern to the new. Enter consultants.

Consultants with or without ability have been hired in droves. This has been money wasted in some cases, but money returned expo-

Life Prescription

nentially in others, depending on the skill of the consultant. Unfortunately, no good criteria exist to tell businessmen which consultant is good for their company, and which is not. As a result, downsizing has been an experimental process, as companies have problem-solved how to do it while dealing with people's lives. Pattern result: a lot of noise and movement without much change.

Personnel Selection

On a more individual level, a company chooses to use a personality test to hire employees. On the surface this action is plausible: knowing what you are getting and how people will fit into your company is a reasonable process. Trying to control the pattern, a company hires all one "type" of person as rated on the test. The outcome for the company is no new information, little conflict, and few diverse opinions. This is great for an operation without much competition. But a company trying to gain a competitive edge doesn't need all the same type of people with pretty much all the same opinions. Pattern result: people think the same so the company stays the same.

Minorities

What about the pattern between whites and minorities? Minorities have complained for years that the "system" is not fair. Guess what? They're right. We have never problem-solved integration. Each new ethnic group that enters our society is cursed with the need to formulate its own political equality by lobbying. They solve the problem with the system by becoming part of the system, but it is a system that has never fully decided what it will do with them.

The result is an interesting dance. The "establishment" must walk on egg shells and speak politically correct language or the minority uses the media to embarrass them and remove public figures from office. This forces political figures to refrain from stating their true feelings anywhere to the public. But the problem is not solved just because we do not talk about it. It merely goes underground. When the problem does emerge, people's outrage is quenched by a mediocre accommodation—a grant, a scholarship program, a library. Pattern result: the same people have the same arguments and make the same deals.

Drugs

What about the war on drugs? The greatest nation in the world, a nation that can intimidate international terrorists, cannot stop the smuggling of drugs? I once talked to a dealer who told me that drug sales could be stopped, *if* the government wanted to. All it had to do was follow the money. The money would lead to the people who finance drugs. But the dealer's opinion was that the government would not want to embarrass itself by arresting the people it found at the end of the trail.

Is there a pattern to drug use in America? Of course, there is! Are there people who know the pattern and could explain it to others to get it stopped? Yes! Why do we not ask them, and give them the laws to attack the problem? Pattern result: more kids learn that it is easier to make $300 a day dealing than $4 an hour working.

The "Big Picture" is the essence of patterns. It is the mastery of problem-solving, the recognition of problems as they exist, the discomfort with ill-fitting solutions, and the search for answers before a situation is life-threatening. Every person has the capacity to use his problem-solving skills to create harmony and success. No one has the right to remove the power of choice from others. We are all charged to find solutions to problems society faces—population increase, government insolvency, violence. But first, we must start with ourselves.

To close, I will describe a project that works with juvenile offenders and whose success is due entirely to the efforts of a handful of county workers and a judge who refused to remain blind to a growing problem and accepted a pattern change as a remedy.

In 1990, the juvenile offender problem in this county was becoming out of hand. The caseload was escalating at an alarming rate. Several alternatives had been instituted. Outdoor therapeutic programs were used for difficult children, group clubs offered after-school programs (individual counseling and group counseling), and schools had multiple programs for youthful offenders. Newly instituted programs had a "honeymoon," short-term effect on the offenders. Recidivism (relapse to crime) was between 50 and 80 percent (not counting juveniles who left the system for adult probation or prisons). Juvenile violent crime was on the rise everywhere. What could one small county do?

Reviewing its program, the county found ways to improve the focus, the specificity of the operation, and the consistency of staff action. Once the design was put into place, the county court was able to reduce caseload, recidivism (18 percent over eighteen months), and juvenile crime. These improvements were so dramatic that the county fathers had trouble accepting them. Rather than being honored for its success, the court was given other agencies' work to do. It was told to embark on a new initiative with unsuccessful programs. This coupling dragged the court workers into a mire that reduced their effectiveness. Over time, they could not hold to the pattern that had brought about their success, and eventually their positive numbers slipped.

Why would one governmental agency not welcome the success of another? *The pattern!* If one agency is more successful than another, something must be wrong with the agency's status quo. Therefore, it must bring the successful program down to its level. This is done insidiously by passing work to the challenger until it is hampered back into mediocrity. This is what happened to the court. It was stopped from doing its job by having to do others' jobs. Recently, however, the court is beginning to recover. Its caseload is down and recidivism is being studied for signs of success. Shhh! Don't tell anybody.

No one person or group can make the system change its patterns. Measured, persistent actions come after someone reaches awareness of his real participation in the "big picture." Rarely is system change the result of one person. To that end, I want to invite and challenge everyone who reads this book to join us in our mission. We feel that

The Big Picture

it is critical to teach people how to interact in a healthy way, to offer them our healthy interaction, and to support them as they independently work on their own health. In part, we accomplish this mission by teaching people to understand themselves as healthy, problem-solving children who have decision-making power over their lives.

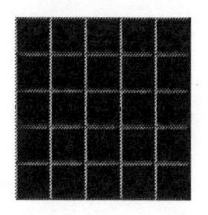

References

Bandura, A. *Aggression: A Social Learning Analysis.* Englewood Cliffs, New Jersey: Prentice-Hall, Inc., 1973.

Boring, E. *A History of Experimental Psychology,* 2nd Edition. Englewood Cliffs, New Jersey: Prentice Hall, Inc., 1950.

Bredemeier, H., and R. Stephenson. *The Analysis of Social Systems.* New York: Holt, Rinehart, and Winston, Inc., 1962.

Cartwright, D., and A. Zander, eds. *Group Dynamics—Research and Theory.* Evanston, Illinois: Row, Peterson, and Co., 1953.

Dreikurs, R. *Children: The Challenge.* New York: Hawthorne Books, Inc., 1964.

Elkind, D. *A Sympathetic Understanding of the Child Birth to Sixteen.* Boston: Allyn and Bacon, Inc., 1971.

Ellis, H. *Fundamentals of Human Learning and Cognition.* Dubuque: William C. Brown Co. Publishers, 1972.

Erickson, M. *Healing in Hypnosis—The Seminars, Workshops and Lectures of Milton H. Erickson,* Volume 1. New York: Irvington Publishers, Inc., 1983.

———. *Life Reframing in Hypnosis—The Seminars, Workshops, and Lectures of Milton H. Erickson,* Volume 2. New York: Irvington Publishers, Inc., 1985.

Reference List

Fenichel, O. *The Psychoanalytic Theory of Neurosis.* New York: W.W. Norton Co., Inc., 1945.

Fournies, F. *Coaching for Improved Work Performance.* New York: Liberty Hall Press, McGraw-Hill, 1987.

Glaser, B. and A. Strauss. *The Discovery of Grounded Theory: Strategies for Qualitative Research.* New York: Aldine Publishing Co., 1967.

Glasser, W. *Reality Therapy.* New York: Harper and Row Publishers, 1965.

Grinker, R., ed. *Toward a Unified Theory of Human Behavior.* Basic Books, Incorporated, 1956.

Hartmann, H. *Ego Psychology and the Problem of Adaptation.* New York: International University Press, 1975.

Henle, M. *The Selected Papers of Wolfgang Kohler.* New York: Liveright Publishing Corporation, 1971.

Hunt, J., ed. *Personality and the Behavior Disorders: A Handbook Based on Experiential and Clinical Research,* Volumes 1 and 2. New York: The Ronald Press Co., 1944.

Jersild, A., Ph.D. *Child Psychology.* New York: Prentice Hall, Inc., 1941.

Kanner, L., M.D. *Child Psychiatry.* Springfield, Illinois: Charles C. Thomas, Publisher, 1960.

Kelly, G. *The Psychology of Personal Constructs,* Volumes 1 and 2. New York: W.W. Norton Co., Inc., 1955.

Koerner, J. *The Miseducation of American Teachers.* Boston: Houghton Mifflin Co., 1963.

Linton, R. *The Cultural Background of Personality.* New York: Appleton-Century-Crofton, Inc., 1945.

Martin, H., M.D., ed. *The Abused Child: A Multidisciplinary Approach to Developmental Issues and Treatment.* Cambridge, Massachusetts: Ballinger Publishing Co., 1976.

Mauldin, J. and D. Elliott. *Success with Children: A Dynamic Socialization Approach to Teaching.* Owensboro, Kentucky: John Mauldin Publishers, 1986.

Mowrer, O. *Learning Theory and Behavior.* New York: John Wiley and Sons, 1960.

Reference List

Murphy, M. *Golf in the Kingdom*. New York: Penguin Books, 1972.

Naisbitt, J. *Megatrends: Ten New Directions Transforming Our Lives*. New York: Warner Books, 1982.

O'Hanlon, W. *Tap Roots: The Underlying Principles of Milton Erickson's Therapy and Hypnosis*. New York: W.W. Norton Co., Inc., 1987.

Payne, W., Ph.D., L.L.D. *Rousseau's Emile or Treatise on Education*. New York: D. Appleton and Co., 1905.

Peikoff, L. *Objectivism: The Philosophy of Ayn Rand*. Middlesex, England: Penguin Books, Ltd., 1991.

Perls, F. *Gestalt Therapy Verbatim*. New York: Bantam Books, 1974.

Rapaport, D. *Organization and Pathology of Thought*. New York: Columbia University Press, 1965.

Redl, F. and D. Wineman. *Controls from Within: Techniques for the Treatment of the Aggressive Child*. Glencoe, Illinois: The Free Press, 1952.

Reynolds, D. *Morita Psychotherapy*. Berkley: University of California Press, 1976.

Rossi, E., and M. Ryan, eds. *Mind-Body Communication in Hypnosis—The Seminars, Workshops and Lectures of Milton H. Erickson*, Volume 3. New York: Irvington Publishers, 1986.

Sasserath, V., ed. *Minimizing High Risk Parenting: A Review of What is Known and Considered Patient of Appropriate Intervention*. Sponsored by Johnson and Johnson Baby Products Co., 1983.

Schlein, S. *A Way of Looking at Things—Selected Papers from 1930 to 1980, Erick H. Erickson*. New York: W.W. Norton and Co., 1987.

Schmuck, R., and P. Schmuck. *Group Processes in a Classroom*. Dubuque: William C. Brown Co. Publishers, 1971.

Sears, J. *Classroom Organization and Control*. Boston: Houghton Mifflin Co., 1928.

Selye, H. *The Stress of Life*. New York: McGraw-Hill Book Co., Inc., 1956.

Shepherd, C. *Small Groups—Some Sociological Perspectives*. San Francisco: Chandler Publishing Co., 1964.

Spock, B., M.D. *Problems of Parents*. Boston: Houghton Mifflin Co., 1962.

Reference List

Thoresen, C., ed. *Behavior Modification in Education,* 72nd Yearbook of the National Society for the Study of Education. Chicago: The University of Chicago Press, 1972.

Usher, A. *A History of Mechanical Inventions.* Cambridge: Harvard University Press, Revised edition, 1954.

Wittenberg, R. *The Art of Group Discipline—A Mental Hygiene Approach to Leadership.* New York: Association Press, 1951.

Woodworth, Robert S. *Psychology,* 4th Edition. New York: Henry Holt and Co., 1945.